The Global Course of the Information Revolution

Recurring Themes and Regional Variations

T0195521

Richard O. Hundley

Robert H. Anderson

Tora K. Bikson

C. Richard Neu

Prepared for the
National Intelligence Council

National Defense Research Institute

RAND

The research described in this report was sponsored by the National Intelligence Council. The research was conducted in RAND's National Defense Research Institute, a federally funded research and development center supported by the Office of the Secretary of Defense, the Joint Staff, the unified commands, and the defense agencies under Contract DASW01-01-C-0004.

Library of Congress Cataloging-in-Publication Data

The global course of the information revolution : recurring themes and regional variations / Richard O. Hundley ... [et al.].
       p. cm.
       "MR-1680."
       ISBN 0-8330-3424-3 (pbk.)
       1. Information superhighway. 2. Information technology. 3. Digital communications. 4. Information society. I. Hundley, Richard O.

   ZA3225.G56 2003
   004.67'8—dc21

                                                                   2003008812

Published 2003 by RAND
1700 Main Street, P.O. Box 2138, Santa Monica, CA 90407-2138
1200 South Hayes Street, Arlington, VA 22202-5050
201 North Craig Street, Suite 202, Pittsburgh, PA 15213-1516
RAND URL: http://www.rand.org/
To order RAND documents or to obtain additional information,
contact Distribution Services: Telephone: (310) 451-7002;
Fax: (310) 451-6915; Email: order@rand.org

RAND has just completed a multiyear effort, sponsored by the National Intelligence Council (NIC), to explore the future of the information revolution throughout the world.[1] This was a multidisciplinary effort with a broad range of participants from both inside and outside RAND, with an overarching goal of mapping the likely future of the global information revolution over the next one to two decades.

This report focuses on the many findings of this study.

This effort included a series of international conferences on specific aspects of the information revolution, involving experts in various relevant areas. The proceedings of these conferences have been documented in the following RAND publications:

Richard O. Hundley, Robert H. Anderson, Tora K. Bikson, James A. Dewar, Jerrold Green, Martin Libicki, and C. Richard Neu, *The Global Course of the Information Revolution: Political, Economic, and Social Consequences—Proceedings of an International Conference*, CF-154-NIC, 2000.

Robert H. Anderson, Philip S. Antón, Steven C. Bankes, Tora K. Bikson, Jonathan Caulkins, Peter J. Denning, James A. Dewar, Richard O. Hundley, and C. Richard Neu, *The Global Course of the Infor-*

---

[1]This effort, conducted during 1999–2002, was carried out in support of the Information Revolution initiative of the Director of Central Intelligence's Strategic Estimates Program.

mation Revolution: Technology Trends—Proceedings of an International Conference, CF-157-NIC, 2000.

Gregory F. Treverton and Lee Mizell, *The Future of the Information Revolution in Latin America: Proceedings of an International Conference*, CF-166-1-NIC, 2001.

Richard O. Hundley, Robert H. Anderson, Tora K. Bikson, Maarten Botterman, Jonathan Cave, C. Richard Neu, Michelle Norgate, and Renée Cordes, *The Future of the Information Revolution in Europe: Proceedings of an International Conference*, CF-172-NIC, 2001.

In addition to these international conferences, separate studies were conducted on the likely course of the information revolution in the Middle East and North Africa, and in the Asia-Pacific region, over the next five to ten years. The results of these studies are documented in the following RAND publications:

Grey E. Burkhart and Susan Older, *The Information Revolution in the Middle East and North Africa*, MR-1653-NIC, 2003.

Nina Hachigian and Lily Wu, *The Information Revolution in Asia*, MR-1719-NIC, 2003.

The findings presented in this report, and in the supporting conference proceedings cited earlier, rely heavily on the views, opinions, and expert judgments of individuals who are knowledgeable regarding the impact and course of the information revolution in their areas of intellectual focus (e.g., technology, business and finance, government, society and culture) and/or their areas of geographic concentration—that is, the experts who participated in the various RAND conferences.[2] These views, opinions, and expert judgments were consensual unless otherwise noted (in this report or in the various conference proceedings). On many key issues, we are not in a position to verify or reject these judgments. They generally do not represent independently verified RAND research conclusions—unless referenced or noted. Nevertheless, RAND took on the challenge of selecting and moderating these discussions as well as pro-

---

[2]For a list of the experts who participated in the various RAND conferences, see the appendix to this report.

viding balance and a level of plausibility and quality assurance to the presented views, opinions, and expert judgments.

This research was sponsored by the NIC and monitored by the National Intelligence Officer (NIO) for Science and Technology. It was conducted by the Acquisition and Technology Policy Center of RAND's National Defense Research Institute (NDRI). NDRI is a federally funded research and development center sponsored by the Office of the Secretary of Defense, the Joint Staff, the defense agencies, and the unified commands.

CONTENTS

Preface   iii

Figures   xix

Tables   xxi

Summary   xxiii

Acknowledgments   xli

Abbreviations   xliii

Chapter One
   INTRODUCTION   1
   We Addressed a Wide Range of Questions   2
      In the Technology Arena   2
      In the Business and Financial Arena   2
      In the Governmental and Political Arena   3
      In the Social and Cultural Arena   3
      With Regard to Regional Variations   4
   Globalization and the Information Revolution Are
      Closely Linked   4
   Some Topics We Did Not Address—Deliberately   5
   The Course of This Effort   5
   This Report   6
   Much Has Happened Since We Began This Effort   7
   Notes   8

PART I. RECURRING THEMES

Chapter Two
NEW TECHNOLOGY DEVELOPMENTS WILL
CONTINUALLY DRIVE THE INFORMATION
REVOLUTION   11
It Is Useful to Distinguish Among Developments in
    Technology, Products, and Services   11
Some Technology Developments Can Be Foreseen   12
Product Developments Will Allow Information
    Devices to Be Ubiquitous, Wearable, and in
    Continuous Contact   13
Services Developments Will Greatly Extend Access to, and
    the Usefulness of, Information Systems   14
    Kiosks Can Provide Easy Access to Some
        Information Services   14
    Entertainment Will Be at the Leading Edge of Novel
        Information Services   15
    Information Services Will Play an Increasing Role in
        Health Care and Telemedicine   16
    Online Education Will Have Increasing, but
        Specialized, Effects   17
    Micropayment Schemes Will Emerge to Handle Small
        Online Payments   17
Markets Will Decide What Possible Products and Services
    Become Actual and Widespread   18
    The Emergence of "Killer Apps" Can Greatly Affect
        Markets and Create Markets   19
Some Tensions Arising from These Developments Will
    Affect the Growth and Spread of IT-Related Products
    and Services.   20
    Optical Communication Technologies Are Highly
        Disruptive to Existing Telecommunication Industries
        Worldwide, and Other New Communications
        Developments Could Be as Well   20
    Open Source Versus Closed Source: Proprietary
        Standards Battles Will Continue   20
    Intellectual Property and Digital Rights Issues Are
        Creating Major Tensions   21

A Period of Information Technology Consolidation Is
  Both Likely and Healthy   21
Notes   22

Chapter Three
THE INFORMATION REVOLUTION IS ENABLING NEW
BUSINESS MODELS THAT ARE TRANSFORMING THE
BUSINESS AND FINANCIAL WORLDS   25
Many New Business Models Are Arising   25
  Electronic Commerce Is Becoming
    Increasingly Important   26
  IT-Driven Changes Are Furthest Along in the
    Financial World   27
  Much of This Leading-Edge, IT-Enabled Business
    Activity Is Concentrated in Geographic "Clusters" . . .   28
  "Creative Destruction" Is a Common Feature of These
    Business and Financial Transformations   28
  Information Work and Information Workers Are
    Becoming Increasingly Important   28
  This IT-Enabled Business and Financial Revolution Will
    Be Ongoing for Some Time   29
  Recent Developments May Temporarily Slow the Pace
    of These Transformations in the Business and
    Financial World and Affect Their Near-Term
    Character, but Not Their Ultimate Magnitude
    and Importance   29
  These Transformations in the Business and Financial
    World Are Changing the Playing Field for
    Governments and Societies   30
Notes   30

Chapter Four
THE INFORMATION REVOLUTION IS AFFECTING
MECHANISMS OF GOVERNANCE AND EMPOWERING
NEW POLITICAL ACTORS   35
Some Traditional Mechanisms of Governance Are
    Becoming Problematic   35
New Governmental Mechanisms Are Being Enabled   36
New Political Actors Are Being Empowered   36
The Information Revolution Could Over Time Change the
    Role of the Nation-State: The Jury Is Still Out   37

Different Nations Will Take Different Approaches to
    Dealing with These Changes   39
The Events of 9/11 May Lead to Increased Governmental
    Intervention into IT Developments   39
Notes   40

Chapter Five
THE INFORMATION REVOLUTION BOTH SHAPES AND
IS SHAPED BY SOCIAL AND CULTURAL VALUES IN
SIGNIFICANT WAYS   45
The Information Revolution Is Being Enabled by
    Technology but Driven Primarily by Nontechnical
    Factors, Including Social and Cultural Factors   45
Digital Divides Within and Between Nations Will Persist,
    but Their Future Scope, Duration, and Significance
    Are Subject to Debate   46
Ability to Acquire and Use Knowledge Will Be Critical for
    Success in the Information Society: Developing
    Human Capital Appropriately Is Key   47
Globalization, Boosted by the Information Revolution,
    Will Continue to Have Multivalenced Social and
    Cultural Effects   49
Will IT-Enabled Globalization Lead to Greater
    Homogeneity or Greater Heterogeneity in
    Sociocultural Terms? The Answer is "Yes" to Both ...   50
The Information Revolution Raises Significant Social-
    Cultural Questions for Which Well-Grounded
    Research Answers Are Unavailable   50
What Is Effective Proximity?   50
What Are Viable Models for Leadership and
    Management in a Networked Global Society?   51
Can the Information Revolution Contribute
    Meaningfully and Measurably to Environmental
    Sustainability?   51
How Should Risk-Tolerance and Long-Term Planning
    Be Balanced over the Course of the Information
    Revolution to Yield Positive Social and Cultural
    Outcomes?   52
Notes   52

Chapter Six
    MANY FACTORS SHAPE AND CHARACTERIZE A
    NATION'S APPROACH TO THE INFORMATION
    REVOLUTION   55
    Some Factors Are Causative   55
        Rich Nations Are Better Positioned Than Poor Nations
            to Exploit the Information Revolution   55
        How a Society Deals with Change Is a Major Factor
            Shaping a Nation's IR Posture   56
        Governments and Laws Can Be Helpful or Unhelpful . .   58
        The Structure of Capital Markets Is Also Important   59
        These Causative Factors Can Play Out in
            Various Ways   59
    Other Factors Are Effects, Not Causes   60
        The Degree and Nature of IT Penetration into a Society
            and the Distribution of Its IT Activity Across the
            Technology, Product, and Service Spectrum Are
            Useful Descriptors of a Nation's IR Posture   60
        Measures of Information Work and Workers and of
            E-Commerce Are Also Important Descriptors   61
        The Presence and Number of IT Business Clusters
            Are Important Descriptors of the Vigor of a Nation's
            IR Posture   61
        The Amount of "Creative Destruction" Going On
            in a Nation Can Be an Important Descriptor of
            Its IR Posture   61
        The Presence of New Political Actors and Changes in
            Governance Are Measures of IR-Induced Change in
            the Political Arena   62
        The Movement of Talented, IT-Trained People Can Be a
            Useful Indicator of a Nation's IR Posture   63
    Notes   63

PART II. REGIONAL VARIATIONS

Chapter Seven
    NORTH AMERICA WILL CONTINUE IN THE VANGUARD
    OF THE INFORMATION REVOLUTION   71

The North American Economy and Society Are
    Well Positioned to Meet the Challenges of the
    Information Revolution   71
North America Will Exploit These Advantages to Continue
    in the Vanguard of the Information Revolution   72
The Dot-Com Crash and Telecom Implosion May Slow
    the Pace of IT-Related Developments in North
    America, but Only Temporarily   73
The Events of 9/11 May Lead to Increased
    Governmental Intervention in IT
    Developments in North America   73
North America Will, in General, Deal Well
    with the Stresses Generated by the
    Information Revolution   74
Notes   75

Chapter Eight
THE INFORMATION REVOLUTION IS FOLLOWING A
SOMEWHAT DIFFERENT AND MORE DELIBERATE
COURSE IN EUROPE   77
Europeans Place More Emphasis on Wireless   77
The Information Revolution in Europe Is Developing in a
    Different Climate   78
    Differing European and American Approaches to
        Economic and Social Change   78
    The Greater Importance Europeans Attach to Economic
        and Social Equity   78
    The European Desire for "Convergence"   78
    Differing Trade-Offs Between Market Forces and
        Government Policies   79
    A Greater European Emphasis on
        Top-Down Planning   79
    The European Emphasis on Sustainability   79
The Course of the Information Revolution in Europe Is
    Somewhat Different   80
Will, or Must, Europe Become More Like America? Maybe
    Yes, Maybe No   81
Some Europeans View American Dominance as Part of
    the "Dark Side" of the Information Revolution   82
Notes   82

Chapter Nine

MANY ASIA-PACIFIC NATIONS ARE POISED TO
DO WELL IN THE INFORMATION REVOLUTION,
SOME ARE NOT   85
Asia-Pacific Nations Vary Greatly in Their Information
    Revolution Postures   85
    Several Asia-Pacific Nations Are Doing Well Today in
        the Information Revolution   85
    Today the Asia-Pacific Region Is a Much More
        Significant Global IT Producer Than a Consumer . . .   86
    Asian Nations Generally Follow the "Japan Model" in
        the Evolution of Their IT Production Activities   87
    Japan Has Something of a "Split Personality" Today
        Regarding the Information Revolution   89
    China and India Are of Special Note as Rapidly
        Emerging IT Users and Producers   90
    Other Asian Nations Are Lagging Well Behind   91
The Impact of the Information Revolution on Politics and
    Governance in the Asia-Pacific Region Varies Widely
    from Nation to Nation   91
    Information Technology Has Had an Impact on Politics
        in Some Asian Nations Thus Far, but Not
        in Others   91
    IT Is Reshaping the Way Asia-Pacific Governments
        Conduct the Business of Governance: More in Some
        Nations Than in Others   92
What Does the Future Hold for the
    Asia-Pacific Region?   93
    Over Time, China Should Emerge as a Major IT Player
        in Asia and the World   93
    Other Asian Nations Currently Leading in IT Will Define
        Their Futures by Their Responses to China's Growing
        IT Role.   94
    Japan's Future Course Is Unclear: It Could Continue as
        a Leader in IT or Gradually Fall Behind   95
    India's Software and Back-Office Service Industries
        Should Prosper; However, a Broader Role in
        the Information Revolution May Be Beyond
        India's Reach   95

Most of Today's Laggards Will Continue to Lag   96
Notes   96

Chapter Ten
LATIN AMERICA FACES MANY OBSTACLES IN
RESPONDING TO THE INFORMATION REVOLUTION:
SOME NATIONS WILL RISE TO THE CHALLENGE,
OTHERS WILL NOT   103
Today Most Latin American Nations Are "Also-Rans" in
    the Information Revolution, as They Are in the
    Global Economy   103
Latin American Nations Can Be Divided into "Leaders,"
    "Successful Outliers," and the Rest   104
    Argentina, Brazil, Chile, Mexico, and Uruguay Have
        Been Latin America's Leaders in the Information
        Revolution in Recent Years   105
    A Few Latin American Nations Are "Successful Outliers"
        Regarding the Information Revolution   106
    The Rest of the Latin American Nations Are Following
        Along Behind—Sometimes Way Behind   107
Latin America Faces Many Obstacles in
    Exploiting Opportunities Offered by
    the Information Revolution   107
What Does the Future Hold for Latin America? Probably
    More of the Same   108
Notes   109

Chapter Eleven
FEW MIDDLE EASTERN AND NORTH
AFRICAN NATIONS WILL FULLY EXPERIENCE
THE INFORMATION REVOLUTION, SOME MAY
MISS IT ALTOGETHER   113
IT Penetration Is Generally Low in Most
    MENA Nations   113
MENA Nations Can Be Grouped into Three Categories
    Regarding the Information Revolution   114
    The "Fearful" Nations   115
    The "Best of Both" Nations   115
    The "Driven" Nations   115
The Social Implications of the Information Revolution for
    the MENA Nations Could Be Wide-Ranging   116

Few MENA Nations Will Fully Exploit the Information
Revolution, Causing This Region to Fall Even Further
Behind OECD Nations   116
The "Driven" Nations   117
The "Best of Both" Nations   118
The "Fearful" Nations   119
Israel   120
Notes   120

Chapter Twelve
MOST COUNTRIES OF SUB-SAHARAN AFRICA
WILL FALL FURTHER BEHIND IN THE
INFORMATION REVOLUTION   125
There Are Extreme Disparities Among African Nations;
As a Result, Few Statements Apply Universally   125
In Africa, Mass Media Predominate over
Point-to-Point Communication   125
Compared with the Rest of the World, Africa Is
Falling Behind   126
Africa's IT Problems Are Not Primarily Technical: They
Involve Factors of Culture, Competence, Capital,
and Control   126
Cultural Factors Complicate and Impede the Spread
and Use of Information Technology in Africa   127
It Takes an Educated Populace to Know How to Bring IT
to Those Who Most Need It   128
Many sub-Saharan Countries Lack Financial and
Physical Capital   128
The Agencies of Control in sub-Saharan African
Countries Often Impede IT Development   129
There Are, However, Positive Indications That
the Information Revolution Is Moving Forward
in Africa   129
External Factors May Indirectly Impede IT
Growth in Africa   130
The HIV/AIDS Epidemic in Africa Affects the Region's
Development Prospects   130
In the Post-9/11 Era, Much of the World's Attention and
Resources Will Be Focused Elsewhere   130
Notes   131

PART III. SOME ADDITIONAL TOPICS (A BRIEF LOOK)

Chapter Thirteen
GEOPOLITICAL TRENDS FURTHERED BY
THE INFORMATION REVOLUTION COULD
POSE CONTINUING CHALLENGES TO THE
UNITED STATES   135
    The U.S. Economy and Society Are Well Poised to Meet
        the Challenges of the Information Revolution   135
    There Are Likely to Be Many Losers or Laggards Elsewhere
        in the World, Some of Whom Could Become
        Seriously Disaffected   135
    The Information Revolution Better Enables
        Disaffected Peoples to Combine and Organize,
        Thereby Rendering Them Powers That Must Be
        Dealt With   136
    The Existence of These Disaffected (and Organized)
        Losers or Laggards Could Lead to Trends in the
        World That May Challenge Vital U.S. Interests   136
        Extreme Losers in the Information Revolution Could
            Become "Failed States"   136
        Responding to the Information Revolution Will Stress
            European Economies, Societies, and Polities,
            Leading to Laggards and Losers Within Europe   136
        The Inability of Japan to Change Sufficiently to Cope
            with the Information Revolution—If This Turns Out
            to Be the Case—Could Lead to the Failure of the
            Japanese Economy   137
    These Trends Would Pose Continuing Challenges to
        U.S. Interests   137
    Notes   137

Chapter Fourteen
WHAT FUTURE EVENTS COULD CHANGE
THESE PROJECTIONS?   139
    Future "Killer Apps," Unclear at Present, Will Determine
        the Precise Nature of IT-Driven Transformations . . .   139
    Many Things Can Slow Down or Speed Up the Pace of IT-
        Driven Transformations   140
    Future Geopolitical Events Could Adversely Affect How
        Different Nations and Regions of the World Fare   140

No Matter What Happens, the Degree to Which
IT Ultimately Changes the World Is Unlikely
to Change 140
Notes 141

Chapter Fifteen
THE INFORMATION REVOLUTION IS PART OF A
BROADER TECHNOLOGY REVOLUTION WITH EVEN
PROFOUNDER CONSEQUENCES 143
Advances in Biotechnology and Nanotechnology Will Also
Greatly Change the World 143
There Are Many Synergies Between IT and These Other
Revolutionary Technologies 144
The Consequences of the Biorevolution Will Be Especially
Profound and Quite Controversial 145
As with the Information Revolution, the Bio- and
Nanorevolutions Will Play Out Unevenly Throughout
the World 145
Notes 145

Appendix
PARTICIPANTS IN THE RAND/NIC INFORMATION
REVOLUTION CONFERENCES 147
References 163

FIGURES

4.1. The Diffusion of Governance in the
21st Century 38
9.1. IT Users and Producers in the
Asia-Pacific Region 86
9.2. The "Japan Model" of the Evolution of
IT Production 88

TABLES

9.1. Sophistication of IT Producers in the
Asia-Pacific Region 89

9.2. Degree of Restrictions on Internet Political Use and
Content, by Type of Government 92

9.3. IT Influence on Politics Versus
Government Type 93

11.1. Countries of the Middle East and North Africa 114

Advances in information technology (IT) are affecting most segments of business, society, and government today in many if not most regions of the world. The changes that IT is bringing about in various aspects of life are often collectively called the "information revolution." RAND has just completed a multiyear effort to explore the nature of these changes throughout the world, painting a picture of the state of the information revolution today and in the near- and mid-term future. (We looked out roughly 5 to 15 years.) This exploration has revealed many common themes that recur throughout the world, as well as many regional variations.

RECURRING THEMES

New Technology Developments Will Continually Drive the Information Revolution

In discussing these developments, we find it useful to distinguish among *technology, products,* and *services.* We view *technology* as the idea or intellectual property based on scientific principles that allows creation of a product that embodies it; wireless communication standards and protocols per se are a technology. A *product* (such as a cellular telephone) may involve hardware and/or software and embodies one or more technologies. *Services* are capabilities offered to users, usually in a form resulting from storage, access, and manipulation of information (by products).

Some *technology* developments can be foreseen, including continued exponential growth in computing power for at least another 10 to 15 years, reaching the foreseeable limits of silicon technology around 2015; continued convergence in voice and data communications and another major leap in available bandwidth during the next two decades; improvements in machine translation so that within 20 years one can have machine translation with any two of three desiderata (high quality, general purpose, fully automatic)—for many purposes and limited domains of discourse, this will be good enough for useful applications; and very strong synergies developing between info-, bio-, nano-, and material technologies.

Product developments will allow information devices to be ubiquitous, wearable, and in continuous contact with one another. We expect to see a multitude of diverse, powerful, inexpensive sensors and other devices capable of (limited-distance) wireless communication; these devices will provide a vastly increased coupling between the physical world and the cyber world, allowing information systems to react much more comprehensively to changes in their environment and vice versa. Computing and information systems will become much more ubiquitous, with convergence of wireless telephones, personal digital assistants (PDAs), radio, voice and email messaging, smart home appliances, etc.; aiding in these developments will be protocols for short-range wireless communication. Display products will undergo dramatic improvement in the coming 15 to 20 years, with "electronic paper" displays that can be rolled or folded and perhaps contain wireless links to personal or other information systems, digital displays that retain their content without requiring power to continually refresh them, and large-screen, flat-panel displays that can be "tiled" to desired sizes.

Services developments will greatly extend access to, and the usefulness of, information systems, with kiosks providing easy access to some information services, entertainment being at the leading edge of novel information services, information services playing an increasing role in health care and telemedicine, online education having increasing but specialized effects, and micropayment schemes emerging to handle small online payments.

It is much easier to predict technology advances than to identify the specific new technology-based products or services that will emerge and be adopted in widespread use. Although technology's progress makes many such products and services possible, markets will decide which possible products and services become actual and widespread; in this process, the emergence of "killer applications" will greatly affect existing markets and create new markets.

Some tensions arising from these developments will affect the growth and spread of IT-related products and services:

- Optical communications technology and Internet Protocol (IP)–based telephony are likely to be highly disruptive to existing telecommunications industries worldwide.

- Open source versus closed source: propriety standards battles will continue.

- Intellectual property and digital rights issues will create major tensions.

A period of IT consolidation, in response to the "dot-com crash" and the implosion of the telecom industry, is both likely and healthy. This consolidation should lead to a stronger foundation for substantial and sustainable IT growth in the coming decades.

We elaborate on these themes in Chapter Two.

The Information Revolution Is Enabling New Business Models That Are Transforming the Business and Financial Worlds

Many new business models enabled by IT are arising, for the internal organization and functioning of business enterprises and for their external interactions with customers, suppliers, and competitors. Many, if not most, of these new external-interaction business models feature one form or another of electronic commerce, which is rising in importance as a major form of economic activity. These IT-driven changes are furthest along in the financial world.

Much of this leading-edge, IT-enabled business activity is concentrated in geographic "clusters," with North America and Europe furthest along in this process, and parts of the Asia-Pacific region following close behind.

"Creative destruction" is a common feature of these business and financial transformations, with new, more-efficient products and services replacing older and less-efficient ones. This process is often, but not always, accompanied by the economic eclipse of the companies producing the old products and services.

"Information work" and "information workers" are becoming an ever-increasing fraction of economic activity and the overall workforce in many nations, as their business and financial worlds undergo the transformations discussed here. Over time, this will free many businesses in "knowledge industries" to relocate to new areas more suited to information work than to manufacturing work, which in turn will affect where people live. This rise in information work will also affect the education required of people, both initially and over their careers. Over time, this should have a significant impact on educational establishments throughout much of the world.

These IT-enabled changes in the business and financial world have been under way for some time, quickening in the past decade. They are furthest along in North America, closely followed by Europe and parts of the Asia-Pacific region. But even in North America, and even more so in other parts of the world, much more is still to come. For the foreseeable future, an unending series of new IT developments will continually drive this ongoing revolution in the business and financial world, along both current and new paths. These transformations in the business and financial world are, in turn, changing the "playing field" for governments and societies.

We elaborate on these themes in Chapter Three.

The Information Revolution Is Affecting Mechanisms of Governance and Empowering New Political Actors

Some traditional mechanisms of governance (e.g., taxation, regulation and licensing) are becoming increasingly problematic as the information revolution allows action beyond the reach of national governments. In these and other areas, governments that are particularly affected will have to find new mechanisms of governance, or create new, near-universal international control structures.

At the same time that some traditional mechanisms of governance are facing challenge, new governmental mechanisms are being enabled, generally falling under the heading of "e-government." This usually involves the use of IT to improve and eventually transform the manner in which governments interact with and provide public services to their citizens, the management of governments' supply chains, and the conduct of internal governmental processes.

New political actors are being empowered by the information revolution—in the business, social, and political realms, at the subnational, transnational, and supranational levels—which is changing the distribution of political power. At the same time, advances in IT are making new Internet-based modes of interaction possible between citizens and their elected representatives, between candidates and voters, and among citizens themselves (when discussing political issues).

Some scholars suggest that the role of the nation-state could change as a result of these developments. For example, a diffusion of governance activities may occur away from the centrality of the nation-state, with some functions migrating to supranational or intergovernmental organizations, some devolving to local governmental units, and some migrating to private market and nonmarket organizations (at the subnational, national, and supranational levels). Others feel that trends in this regard are by no means clear, pointing out the many essential functions that the nation-state will continue to play. Considering these vastly different visions of the future presented by various "experts," one must conclude that the future role of the nation-state in the information age is unclear.

Different nations will take different approaches to dealing with these changes. Smaller nations may more readily give up some prerogatives of the nation-state. Larger nations may be less willing to give up any prerogatives and may try harder to preserve the traditional roles of the nation-state.

We elaborate on these themes in Chapter Four.

The Information Revolution Both Shapes and Is Shaped by Social and Cultural Values in Significant Ways

The information revolution is being enabled by technology but is driven primarily by nontechnical factors, including social and cultural factors. Social and cultural change will have to take place if individuals, organizations, and nations are to fully exploit the capabilities of IT. Unintended consequences will inevitably be produced in this process. Those that arise when social and technical influences combine may well dominate the intended ones.

Digital divides within and between nations will persist, but their future scope, duration, and significance are subject to debate. Within countries, IT diffusion generally exacerbates disparities and reinforces social cleavages, at least until saturation has been achieved. Moreover, the polarization between the rich and the poor is made more acute because of its visibility in the information society. By and large, the same sorts of growing and visible inequalities as a cause and a consequence of differential access to and use of IT are even sharper at the level of national states. While there is reasonable consensus about the present existence of these digital divides, there is also considerable debate over how their implications should be assessed.

The ability to acquire and use knowledge will be critical for success in the information society, as knowledge work constitutes an increasing proportion of all work in the long-term future. Accordingly, developing human capital appropriately is key. A "quality education for all" will be one of the keys to a nation's success in the information age. This presents different challenges in different parts of the world.

Globalization, boosted by the information revolution, will continue to have multivalenced social and cultural effects. While its economic effects are widely recognized, knowledgeable observers also give considerable weight to its societal implications—both positive and negative. These include further widening of the gap between the political/intellectual/economic elites and others in developing nations, and the globalization of entertainment and, consequently, styles (or at least fads), which leads those in some countries to feel that their own national cultures are being vitiated.

The information revolution will stimulate greater homogeneity in the institutional and legal infrastructures of societies networked across nations while at the same time enhancing the heterogeneity of their constituent cultures.

We elaborate on these themes in Chapter Five.

Many Factors Shape and Characterize a Nation's Approach to the Information Revolution

Some of these factors are causative and can play out in various ways:

- Rich nations are better positioned than poor nations to exploit the information revolution (IR).

- How a society deals with change is a major factor shaping a nation's IR posture.

- Governments and laws can be helpful or unhelpful.

- The structure of capital markets is also important.

Other factors are effects, not causes. The following factors add richness to the description of a nation's posture and serve as ways of tracking its performance:

- The degree and nature of IT penetration into a society and the distribution of its IT activity across the technology, product, and service spectrum are useful descriptors of a nation's IR posture.

- The amount of information work, information workers, and e-commerce in a nation also serves as an important descriptor.

- The presence and number of IT business clusters in a nation are important measures of the vigor of a nation's IR posture.

- The amount of "creative destruction" going on in a nation can be another important measure of the vigor of a nation's IR posture.

- The presence of new political actors and changes in governance are measures of IR-induced change in the political arena.

- The movement of talented, IT-trained people can be a useful indicator of a nation's IR posture.

We elaborate on each of these factors in Chapter Six.

REGIONAL VARIATIONS

North America Will Continue in the Vanguard of the Information Revolution

The North American (i.e., U.S. and Canadian) economies and societies are well positioned to meet the challenges of the information revolution. They have many advantages, including well-developed physical infrastructures and human capital; economies and societies that are generally receptive to change; governments that provide an environment generally hospitable to business developments; legal regimes with good intellectual property protections, well-established contract and bankruptcy laws, and strong protections for freedom of expression; and innovative and efficient capital markets with well-developed venture capital communities. Both are nations of immigrants that attract energetic, talented, IT-trained people from all over the world.

North America will exploit these advantages to continue in the vanguard of the information revolution. The dot-com crash and the telecom implosion may slow the pace of IT-related developments in North America, but only temporarily. Further, North America will, in general, deal well with the stresses generated by the information revolution.

We elaborate on the course of the information revolution in North America in Chapter Seven.

The Information Revolution Is Following a Somewhat Different and More Deliberate Course in Europe

In the technology arena, the European view of the information revolution is similar to the American view but with more emphasis placed on wireless technology.

While the technology underpinnings are largely the same, the social, political, and economic climate in which the information revolution is developing in Europe differs in important ways from that in America. These differences include the following:

- Differing European and American approaches to economic and social change, which comes easier in America than in Europe.

- The greater importance that Europeans attach to economic and social equity.

- The European desire for convergence among the nations of Europe insofar as economic prosperity is concerned.

- Differing trade-offs between market forces and government policies, with the United States giving markets more free rein and Europe relying more on governments to produce socially desirable ends.

- A greater European emphasis on top-down planning by governmental and business elites.

As a result of this different climate, the information revolution is following a somewhat different course in Europe than in America, with the Europeans' greater risk aversion causing the creative destruction process to proceed more slowly, the European economic and social equity emphasis leading to a more subdued approach to new IT-related business opportunities, and the top-down planning mentality reinforcing this slower approach. Consequently, up to now, the information revolution has been proceeding more deliberately in Europe than in America, with the United States in the vanguard in most, but not all, IT-related areas and Europe following somewhat behind. This is likely to continue for at least the next few years, if not longer.

We elaborate on the course of the information revolution in Europe in Chapter Eight.

Many Asia-Pacific Nations Are Poised to Do Well in the Information Revolution, Some Are Not

Asia-Pacific nations vary greatly in their information revolution postures. Several are major IT and Internet users, with Internet penetration in South Korea, Hong Kong, Japan, and Australia exceeding even the U.S. level in 2000, and Singapore, Taiwan, and New Zealand not far behind. In contrast to the situation in the United States, however, most Internet usage in Asia today is by businesses—not from the home—and this business usage is not terribly sophisticated.

Japan, Singapore, Taiwan, South Korea, Malaysia, Thailand, and the Philippines are all major IT producers on the world stage, with Asia as a whole accounting for 70 to 80 percent of total world output of a wide range of important IT materials, components, and products. Asian IT producers have generally followed the "Japan model" of progressively sophisticated production technology, beginning with labor-intensive, low-value manufacturing and proceeding to higher-value-added stages. South Korean and Taiwanese companies are among the more technologically advanced and diversified after Japan, but they face challenges on their road to becoming global IT innovators. At the other end of the spectrum, most Southeast Asian IT producers appear to be stagnating at lower rungs on the production ladder.

Japan itself has something of a "split personality" regarding the information revolution. There is no question that it is one of the world's leaders in IT today. However, much has been written in recent years regarding the rigidities of the Japanese society, economy, and government. If this condition persists, it could lead Japan gradually to fall behind the nations in the vanguard of the information revolution. On the other hand, some observers have noted a recent emergence of individualism and entrepreneurship in some sectors of the Japanese IT industry. If this nascent trend persists and spreads, it could ensure the future vitality of that industry, in spite of the rigidities in the larger society. In that case, Japan would continue as a world leader in IT, albeit with an ever-increasing fraction of its manufacturing operations moving to Japanese-owned manufacturing facilities in China. It remains to be seen which of these forces—rigidities in the overall society or nascent individualism and entrepreneurship in the Japanese IT industry—proves stronger.

China is of special note as a rapidly emerging IT producer. Clearly defined clusters of IT industry are already developing there, although IT output is far from being a major component of its economy today. The major driving forces in China are the size and potential of its local market and the almost endless availability of cheap labor, both of which attract foreign investment. In recent years, China has become the IT manufacturing base of choice for Asian, North American, and even European companies—a trend that is not only likely to continue but also accelerate now that China has joined the World Trade Organization. As a corollary, China is also beginning to attract a large, increasingly advanced IT knowledge base, some of it from expatriate Chinese returning home after receiving technical training overseas. As a result, China should continue advancing to later stages in IT industry development and, over time, become a major IT player not only in Asia but also in the world, while in the process possibly leapfrogging many nations that today are more advanced but burdened by the inertia created by legacy infrastructures.

South Korea, Taiwan, and the leading IT nations in Southeast Asia achieved their current positions initially by serving as low-cost manufacturing outposts for North American, European, and Japanese electronics and IT companies and gradually working up the IT value-added chain. This process took several decades. The emergence of China as the new low-cost, mass-market manufacturing outpost of choice in Asia changes the IT playing field on which these other Asian nations must now operate. This will not necessarily be a zero-sum game; China's IT gains do not have to be losses for other Asian nations. For these other nations to survive as viable players in the IT world, they must redefine their business models, carving out value-added niches that can withstand the Chinese onslaught. Some of them may succeed by retaining design and high-level engineering capabilities at home while outsourcing manufacturing operations to China, but others, which have not yet advanced to the design and high-level engineering level in their IT operations, may not.

India has three important advantages in the global IT competition: a plentiful supply of talented IT-trained people; copious numbers of educated, low-cost workers proficient in English; and close ties to the many Indian entrepreneurs in Silicon Valley. As a result, IT business clusters have developed there, it is a world leader in back-office services and software outsourcing, and its software production has increased fiftyfold over the past 10 years. The prosperity and growth of the Indian software and back-office service industries should continue, at least over the near- to mid-term. However, going beyond software into IT hardware activities may be difficult, particularly in view of China's growing role in this area. Also, the entire Indian high-tech industry is a thin veneer on top of the Indian economy. Much of the nation is still in the agricultural age, not yet having reached the industrial age, let alone the information age. These factors may place any broader role in the information revolution beyond India's reach.

Many other Asian nations are lagging well behind today; these include Bhutan, Cambodia, Indonesia, Laos, Mongolia, Myanmar, Nepal, Pakistan, Sri Lanka, Vietnam, and the nations of Central Asia. These nations have low levels of Internet penetration and usage, and little or no IT production activity, and they lack one or more essential elements required to do well in the information revolution. Not only are they lagging behind today, but also little is occurring to improve their future situations insofar as the information revolution is concerned.

We elaborate on the course of the information revolution in the Asia-Pacific region in Chapter Nine.

Latin America Faces Many Obstacles in Responding to the Information Revolution: Some Nations Will Rise to the Challenge, Others May Not

Today, most Latin American nations are "also-rans" in the information revolution, as they are in the global economy. Regarding the information revolution, they can be divided into "leaders," "successful outliers," and the rest.

Argentina, Brazil, Chile, Mexico, and Uruguay have been Latin America's leaders in the information revolution in recent years, leading Latin America in most measures of IT-penetration and usage and in IT-related business and financial developments, and providing IT-related leadership examples to the rest of Latin America. Of these nations, Mexico and Chile continue to do well today, whereas Argentina, Uruguay, and Brazil have recently suffered financial difficulties—in Argentina's case, grave difficulties—that put future economic and IT development in jeopardy.

Several of the small island states in the Caribbean—including the Cayman Islands, the Bahamas, St. Barts, Aruba, the British Virgin Islands, and the U.S. Virgin Islands—are successful outliers regarding the information revolution today. These nations have per capita incomes that are among the highest in Latin America and are much further along in IT penetration and use. They share several preconditions: their governments are founded on trust and transparency; they have a well-established rule of law, high literacy rates, economic cultures in which business can prosper, populations fluent in English, and, perhaps most importantly, political stability. In Central America, Costa Rica is another IT outlier. Intel has based an assembly plant there, which has had a major impact on Costa Rican employment and growth. In attracting Intel, Costa Rica had advantages similar to the Caribbean islands. Even though they are doing well themselves in the information revolution, because they are small and removed geographically from the mainstream of Latin America, Costa Rica and these Caribbean nations do not provide leadership examples to the rest of Latin America; they are information revolution outliers, not leaders.

The rest of the Latin American nations lag behind these leaders and successful outliers, often way behind. The situation is particularly dire for the nations on the Andean ridge (e.g., Bolivia, Ecuador, Peru), those torn by internal guerrilla conflicts (e.g., Colombia), and impoverished island nations of the Caribbean (e.g., Haiti).

Latin America faces many obstacles in exploiting opportunities offered by the information revolution, including a government role in the economy that is often more of an impediment than an advantage in many Latin American nations; privileged positions for large, old-economy firms that often impede the development of markets by new IT-related firms; a financial system in many nations that is not conducive to IT-related startups; shortages of skilled people because of deficiencies in the educational systems and "brain drain" losses, primarily to North America; a pronounced digital divide, even in the leading Latin American nations; and a propensity for frequent financial crises.

All in all, the business and social climate in Latin America is much less hospitable to the information revolution than in North America or Europe, or in many parts of Asia. As a result, the gap between this region and the world's IT leaders is, in the view of experts, not likely to close.

We elaborate on the course of the information revolution in Latin America in Chapter Ten.

Few Middle Eastern and North African Nations Will Fully Experience the Information Revolution, Some May Miss It Altogether

With a few notable exceptions—Bahrain, Israel, Kuwait, Qatar, and the United Arab Emirates (UAE)—IT penetration is below world averages in most Middle Eastern and North African (MENA) nations, sometimes well below. Moreover, irrespective of its magnitude, the pattern of IT diffusion and use in the region is irregular, favoring the wealthy and privileged. This could increase the economic and social disparities between the richest and poorest sectors of MENA societies as time goes on.

The MENA nations can be grouped into three categories regarding the information revolution: "fearful," "driven," and "best of both." The fearful nations include Algeria, Iraq, Libya, and Syria, countries that have limited Internet connectivity or have prohibited it altogether; they would rather forgo the potential benefits in order to ensure that they avoid any negative consequences of joining the networked world. The "best of both" nations are Iran, Saudi Arabia, Tunisia, and the UAE, each of which has tried to develop a tightly controlled domestic Internet network that will enable it to reap benefits in commerce, academia, and government while keeping a close watch and maintaining strict limits on what can and cannot be done and what kinds of information are available.

The rest of the MENA nations can be characterized as "driven." They want what the information revolution offers, and want it badly enough to be willing to risk some disbenefits that may arise from more open and possibly "unacceptable" communications. The wealthiest of these countries, including Bahrain, Kuwait, and Qatar, have well-developed information infrastructures. The poorest country, Yemen, has achieved very little. The middle-tier countries (Egypt, Jordan, Lebanon, Morocco, and Oman) have made interesting but unexceptional progress.

Regarding the future, with the exception of Israel, which we discuss separately below, only a few MENA nations—principally Bahrain, Kuwait, Qatar, and the UAE—are likely to fully exploit opportunities offered by the information revolution. Most of the others will lag behind because of inadequate physical infrastructures and human capital, governmental policies that hinder development, or cultural impediments, causing this region to fall even further behind the Organisation for Economic Cooperation and Development (OECD) nations.

As with most everything else in the MENA region, Israel is a special case insofar as the information revolution is concerned. During the latter half of the 1990s, Israel developed a venture capital industry, with investment capital flowing into the country from elsewhere in the world, particularly from the United States. As a result, in early 2000 before the current intifada started, the number of Israeli startup firms per capita was the highest anywhere in the world except for Silicon Valley, and the nation ranked third in the world in the number of NASDAQ-listed companies. This led to Israeli strengths in a number of IT areas, including Internet telephony, an industry largely erected upon Israeli innovations. These were among Israel's strengths in 2000. Since then, the intifada has put all this at risk. Clearly, Israel's future as a world player in the information revolution is held at least partially hostage to the outcome of the Arab-Israeli peace process.

We elaborate on the course of the information revolution in the MENA region in Chapter Eleven.

Most Countries of sub-Saharan Africa Will Fall Further Behind in the Information Revolution

There are extreme disparities among African nations; as a result, few statements apply universally. As one example of these disparities, South Africa has roughly half of the continent's IT infrastructure, Nigeria and the North African region each have about one-sixth, and all the rest of Africa accounts for only one-sixth of the infrastructure. Even excluding South Africa, there are also dramatic disparities among the northern, eastern, western, and southern African regions, and within countries of those regions.

With those caveats, there are several measures that help place Africa in context. First, mass media (i.e., radio and television) are now, and will remain for the next decade or so at least, the predominant information dissemination media in Africa. For every telephone in Africa, there are 2,500 televisions and 14,000 radios. Compared with the rest of the world, Africa is far behind in per capita telephone subscribers. Regarding Internet access, in 1998 Africa had just 4 percent of the world's Internet hosts and 0.22 percent of World Wide Web sites, with more than half of these being in South Africa, even though it has 12 percent of the world's population. One must also remember how poor Africa is in general: The wealthiest 15 individuals in the world, taken together, have a greater net worth than all of sub-Saharan Africa.

Africa's IT problems are not primarily technical; they involve the following factors of culture, competence, capital, and control:

- Cultural factors such as language, nationalism, stratification, legal framework, vertical authority relationships, trust, meritocracy, and concept of information complicate and impede the spread and use of information technology in Africa.

- It takes an educated populace to know how to bring IT to those who most need it. Africa is lacking in this area.

- In many sub-Saharan countries, financial and physical capital (electric power and telecommunications) are lacking.

- The agencies of control in sub-Saharan African countries—governments, militaries, religious organizations, the private sector— often impede IT development.

In spite of these impediments, there are positive indications that the information revolution is moving forward in Africa. However, two additional factors may indirectly impede progress:

- The HIV/AIDS epidemic in Africa, which has become the biggest threat to the continent's development.

- In the post-9/11 era, much of the world's attention and resources will be focused elsewhere.

For all these reasons, it is likely that information technology improvements will continue in Africa, but the region will continue to fall further behind much of the rest of the world during the next several decades.

We elaborate on the course of the information revolution in sub-Saharan Africa in Chapter Twelve.

SOME ADDITIONAL TOPICS (A BRIEF LOOK)

Geopolitical Trends Furthered by the Information Revolution Could Pose Continuing Challenges to the United States

While the U.S. economy and society are well poised to meet the challenges of the information revolution, there are likely to be many losers and laggards elsewhere in the world. Many of these losers or laggards will become disaffected—some seriously.

The information revolution better enables disaffected peoples to combine and organize, thereby rendering them powers that must be dealt with—in many, but not all, cases.

The existence of these disaffected and organized losers or laggards could lead to trends in the world that may challenge vital U.S. interests. For example:

- Extreme losers in the information revolution could become "failed states." Such failed states could become breeding grounds for terrorists, who could threaten vital U.S. interests.

- Responding to the information revolution will stress European economies, societies, and politics, leading to laggards and losers within Europe. This could over time put increasing stress on the North Atlantic Alliance.

- The inability of Japan to change sufficiently to cope with the information revolution—if this turns out to be the case—could lead to the failure of the Japanese economy. The failure of Japan's economy would in turn lead to a vacuum in Asia likely to be filled by China. This would greatly enhance China's position within Asia and make it more likely that China becomes a peer competitor of the United States.

These trends would pose continuing challenges to U.S. interests.

We expand on these thoughts in Chapter Thirteen.

What Future Events Could Change These Projections?

Future "killer applications," unclear at present, will determine the precise nature of IT-driven transformations. They are the wild cards that will determine the fine details of the information revolution.

Many elements can slow down or speed up the pace of IT-driven transformations. Adverse financial events can slow things down; unexpected killer applications can speed things up. Such unpredictable events will occur in the future just as they have in the past.

Future geopolitical events—such as a new "cold war," a global military conflict, or a large-scale regional conflict—could adversely affect how different nations and regions of the world perform. Persistent, widespread, devastating terrorist incidents could have the same effect on a nation or region.

No matter what happens, however, the degree to which IT eventually transforms the world is unlikely to change. We expect these changes ultimately to be profound.

We expand on these thoughts in Chapter Fourteen.

The Information Revolution Is Part of a Broader Technology Revolution with Even Profounder Consequences

The information revolution is not the only technology-driven revolution under way in the world today but merely the most advanced. Advances in biotechnology and nanotechnology, and their synergies with IT, should also change the world greatly over the course of the 21st century.

The consequences of the biorevolution will be especially profound and quite controversial. The ability to alter plant and animal genomes has already led to considerable controversy; the ability to alter the human genome will lead to enormous controversy.

We expand on these thoughts in Chapter Fifteen.

ACKNOWLEDGMENTS

The results presented here draw heavily on the contributions of the participants in the four RAND/NIC information revolution conferences. Their names are listed in the Appendix. They all deserve a major vote of thanks.

We also draw on the contributions of the participants in the 2001 NIC/State Department conference on the information revolution in Africa. They also deserve our thanks.

Special thanks are due to Grey Burkhart and Susan Older, who wrote the report on the course of the information revolution in the Middle East and North Africa, and to Nina Hachigian and Lily Wu, who wrote a similar report on the course of the information revolution in the Asia-Pacific region.

Our RAND colleagues William Overholt and Philip Antón reviewed a draft of this report and made many valuable comments.

Finally, thanks are also due to Lawrence Gershwin, National Intelligence Officer for Science and Technology, without whose vision and support this project would not have accomplished what it has, and to Brian Shaw, Deputy National Intelligence Officer for Science and Technology, for valuable feedback throughout the course of this effort.

ABBREVIATIONS

1G	first generation
2G	second generation
3G	third generation
AHDR	Arab Human Development Report
B2B	business-to-business
B2C	business-to-consumer
DRAM	dynamic random access memory
GDP	gross domestic product
HIV/AIDS	Human Immunodeficiency Virus/ Acquired Immune Deficiency Syndrome
HTML	Hyper Text Markup Language
IC	integrated circuit
IP	Internet Protocol
IR	information revolution
ISP	Internet Service Provider
IT	information technology
"killer apps"	killer applications
MEMS	microelectromechanical systems
MENA	Middle East and North Africa

NIC	National Intelligence Council
OECD	Organisation for Economic Cooperation and Development
PC	personal computer
PCIPB	The President's Critical Infrastructure Protection Board
PDA	personal digital assistant
SRAM	static random access memory
UAE	United Arab Emirates
UNAIDS	Joint United Nations Programme on HIV/AIDS
Wi-Fi	wireless fidelity

Chapter One

INTRODUCTION

Advances in information technology (IT) are affecting most segments of business, society, and government in many if not most regions of the world. The changes that IT is bringing about in various aspects of life are often collectively called the "information revolution."[1] Many of these changes could over time prove to be profound; some may have already done so. A wide range of national and international political, economic, and societal issues arise from these changes, both now and in the future.

Understanding the various impacts that advances in IT will have and the likely nature of future changes that IT will bring about, in different societies all around the world, and the issues (i.e., problems and opportunities) that will arise from these impacts and changes is very important—and also quite difficult. It is important because IT is likely to change the 21st-century world just as much as the steam engine, railroad, and telegraph changed the 19th-century world, and just as much as electricity, the internal combustion engine, automobile and airplane, and the telephone, radio, and television changed the 20th-century world.[2] It is difficult because, while the technology developments that enable and drive the information revolution are more or less the same throughout the world, a large number of factors—social and cultural, political and governmental, business and financial—shape each society's approach to those technology developments. These factors interact in a variety of ways, both straightforward and subtle, and are subject to numerous variations in nations throughout the world, leading to many different national or regional manifestations of the information revolution.

RAND has conducted a multiyear effort, sponsored by the National Intelligence Council (NIC), to explore this important, difficult subject: the likely future of the information revolution throughout the world—in this case, over the next one to two decades.[3] This was a multidisciplinary effort with a broad range of participants from both inside and outside RAND. This report summarizes what was learned in this effort.

WE ADDRESSED A WIDE RANGE OF QUESTIONS

In charting the likely future of the information revolution, we addressed a wide range of questions, such as the following.

In the Technology Arena

- What advances in information technology will the world see in the next 10 to 20 years?

- How broad and deep will IT penetration be in various regions of the world?

- What are the main factors driving advances in IT?

In the Business and Financial Arena

- How will IT affect business and financial developments over the next 10 to 20 years (e.g., new methods of work, e-commerce, new business models, new paradigms for financial services)?

- What are the sources of financing for IT and for new IT-enabled businesses and services? How do these vary from one nation to another?

- How open are various countries to foreign investment and foreign roles in IT-related business?

- Who are the major players in these business and financial developments? Are they predominantly national, regional, or global?

- What characteristics of the business environment in various countries facilitate or inhibit growth in the use of IT and in new

IT-enabled businesses? What are the driving forces of change? What are the main obstacles?

- How are issues of intellectual property, encryption, standards, commercial and contract law, and the like being dealt with in businesses created or transformed by IT? What are the main differences across countries?

- Ultimately, what can be said about the impact of IT on the conduct of business and economic advance in various nations and regions?

In the Governmental and Political Arena

- How different are the approaches of various governments in fostering, channeling, regulating, or inhibiting the spread of IT?

- How may governance change in the information age (e.g., changes in the role of the nation-state, rise of new political actors)?

- Will IT facilitate the creation of nongovernmental organizations?

- How may politics be affected by IT? What is the future for "digital democracy"?

- Is information technology likely to spur political integration, disintegration, or both?

In the Social and Cultural Arena

- What social and cultural changes may the information revolution bring about (e.g., social impacts of increasing disparities and the "digital divide," impact of the information revolution on national or regional social and cultural values, e-learning)?

- Is the information revolution increasing economic inequalities within or between nations? Is it increasing social inequalities in this or other ways—for instance, by accentuating rural-urban cleavages?

- How will IT affect the delivery of human service over the next decade? How will it change health care, education, and other social services? How, if at all, will it change the balance between public and private providers? What will be the implications of these changes?

- What social or cultural factors prominent in one nation/region or another facilitate or inhibit the diffusion of IT and advances in IT-related industries? How common are these factors in various areas of the world?

With Regard to Regional Variations

- How do all of the above vary from one nation to another, from one part of the world to another?

- Which countries are leading, which lagging in IT developments? What are the predominant differences across countries (and within them)?

- Broadly speaking, how do the projections of IT patterns vary from one region of the world to another? Where do various regions fall on the spectrum of private-sector-dominated, bottom-up versus public-sector-driven, top-down IT-related development?

- What are the key factors in or determinants of how the information revolution plays out in each major region of the world?

GLOBALIZATION AND THE INFORMATION REVOLUTION ARE CLOSELY LINKED

In addressing these and similar questions, the effects of the information revolution are commingled with those of globalization—the rapid advance in cross-border integration in many areas of economic and other human activities that has been ongoing for some time, facilitated by advances in transportation systems and communications systems and by the elimination of regulatory barriers to the movement of money, goods, services, and people. Globalization and the information revolution are closely linked. Indeed, advances in IT are one of the principal enablers of globalization. Conversely, globalization is shaping the world in which the information revolution is playing out.

In most cases it is difficult, and in some cases impossible, to separate the effects of the information revolution from those of globalization. In almost all cases, it serves little useful purpose to do so. Accordingly, in what follows we treat the information revolution and globalization as intimately commingled phenomena, the effects of which we do not attempt to separate.

SOME TOPICS WE DID NOT ADDRESS—DELIBERATELY

There were some aspects of the information revolution that we did not address, at least not in any detail. The two most important are

- The security issues raised by advances in IT, or more precisely, by the ever-increasing fraction of human economic, political, social, and other societal activity that is carried out via information systems and networks. This subject is sometimes referred to as "security in cyberspace."

- The impact of advances in information technology on military operations, sometimes referred to as the "revolution in military affairs."

We did not address these topics primarily because they already have been covered by other investigators at considerable breadth and great depth.[4] To cover them again in our study would have duplicated previous work; we judged that our resources could be better spent elsewhere.

THE COURSE OF THIS EFFORT

This effort included a series of international conferences on specific aspects of the information revolution, involving experts in various relevant areas, as well as selected in-depth studies. The first step in this effort was a conference held in November 1999 on the political, economic, social, and cultural trends driven by the information revolution as they manifest themselves globally; the proceedings of this conference were published in Hundley et al. (2000). The second step was a conference held in May 2000 to explore the technological drivers of the revolution in more detail; the proceedings of that conference were published in Anderson et al. (2000). The third step was a conference on the information revolution in Latin America, conducted in November 2000; the proceedings of that conference were published in Treverton and Mizell (2001). The fourth step was a conference on the future of the information revolution in Europe, held in Belgium in April 2001; the proceedings of that conference were published in Hundley et al. (2001).

In addition to these conferences conducted by RAND under NIC sponsorship, this effort has also benefited from an international conference on the information revolution in Africa conducted by the NIC and the State Department Bureau of Intelligence and Research in October 2001.[5]

To complement these international conferences, separate studies were conducted on the course of the information revolution in the Asia-Pacific region and in the Middle East and North Africa.[6] The results of these studies are reported in Hachigian and Wu (2003) and in Burkhart and Older (2003), respectively.

These international conferences and in-depth studies are the primary body of information on which this report is based and are supplemented by the many source documents listed in the References.

THIS REPORT

This report represents a final integration and summing up of all the findings of RAND's multiyear effort to chart the worldwide course of the information revolution.[7] It is organized in three parts:

- **Part I** sets out common themes that recur throughout the world—with separate chapters on the technology dimension of the information revolution (Chapter Two); the business/financial dimension (Chapter Three); the government/political dimension (Chapter Four); and the social/cultural dimension (Chapter Five), as well as a chapter on the factors that distinguish one region or nation from another insofar as their approach to the information revolution is concerned (Chapter Six).

- **Part II** discusses regional variations in these themes, as the information revolution proceeds differently in different regions of the world—with separate chapters on the future course of the information revolution in North America[8] (Chapter Seven); the future course of the information revolution in Europe (Chapter Eight); the information revolution in the Asia-Pacific region (Chapter Nine); the information revolution in Latin America (Chapter Ten); the information revolution in the Middle East and North Africa (Chapter Eleven); and the information revolution in sub-Saharan Africa (Chapter Twelve).

• **Part III** takes a brief look at some additional topics emerging during the course of our work: Chapter Thirteen outlines geopolitical trends furthered by the information revolution that could pose continuing challenges to the United States. Chapter Fourteen addresses the question of what future events could change the projections we make here. And Chapter Fifteen mentions the broader technology revolution of which the information revolution is but one part; this broader revolution should over time have even profounder consequences than those of the information revolution taken by itself.[9]

Insofar as format is concerned, each of the chapters of this report is written (as much as possible) as a stand-alone piece that can be read on its own, without reference to the other chapters. Notes are placed at the end of each chapter, rather than at the bottom of each page, so as not to break up the reading process (for those who do not want to get into the details presented in the notes).

MUCH HAS HAPPENED SINCE WE BEGAN THIS EFFORT

This effort began in mid-1999, before the worst of the dot-com crash and the telecom implosion. All of the international conferences that were a major part of the effort, and on which we base many of the findings of our study, were conducted before the events of September 11, 2001. These events—the dot-com and telecom crashes and September 11—clearly changed the world. The question is, How will this changed world affect the future course of the information revolution?

In the chapters that follow, we comment on what impact we feel these events will have on the future development of the information revolution—on either the character or pace of that development, over either the short or long term.

NOTES

[1]This is not the first "information revolution" that humans have experienced. The invention of moveable-type printing, in the 15th century in Europe and earlier in China, was one. The invention of writing several millennia ago was another. (This may have been the greatest information revolution of them all.) And there have been other inventions classified by some as information revolutions as well (e.g., the invention of the telegraph, the telephone). While recognizing these earlier revolutions, this report concentrates on the current one. (See Dewar, 1998, for a discussion of possible parallels between the invention of the printing press and the current information revolution.)

[2]Information technology is not the only technology that will change the 21st-century world. Biotechnology, nanotechnology, materials sciences, and their synergies with IT should also transform the world greatly (see Antón, Silberglitt, and Schneider, 2001). We come back to this issue in Chapter Fifteen.

[3]This effort was carried out in support of the Information Revolution initiative of the Director of Central Intelligence's Strategic Estimates Program.

[4]PCIPB (2002) provides an overview of the present state of security (and insecurity) in cyberspace. Hundley (1999) discusses the current "revolution in military affairs," placing it in the historical context of past military revolutions.

[5]The results of this conference on the information revolution in Africa are reported on in NIC/State Department (2002).

[6]RAND originally planned to hold an international conference in Asia on the course of the information revolution in the Asia-Pacific region. In the post–September 11, 2001 environment, this was no longer advisable.

[7]This report is a *summary*. As such, it cannot include all the supporting detail contained in the various conference proceedings and other supplementary materials cited in the References (at the end of this report), which should be consulted for additional justification and discussion of points made in this summary.

[8]By *North America*, we mean here the United States and Canada. Mexico is discussed as part of Latin America.

[9]Part III is definitely a *brief* look at these issues, meant merely to introduce the subjects.

PART I. RECURRING THEMES

Chapter Two

NEW TECHNOLOGY DEVELOPMENTS WILL CONTINUALLY DRIVE THE INFORMATION REVOLUTION

It is clear that many current information technology trends will continue, at least over the next 15 to 20 years: computing will get faster and cheaper; communication bandwidth will increase; interesting new products (beyond cell phones and handheld personal information managers, or perhaps a merging of the two) will emerge—and so on. And yet, many previous attempts to forecast future technology developments have been woefully lacking, if not just plain wrong. Perhaps more importantly, it is difficult to predict the adoption and widespread use of various IT-enabled products and services, especially when their success depends on a critical mass of usage. Twenty years ago, circa 1983, essentially no one predicted the explosive development of the World Wide Web—indeed, although a precursor of the Internet was a fairly robust technology, there was no HTML, nothing like today's "chat rooms," and no gigahertz multigigabyte laptop computers or cell phones. And no one knows what the next "killer app" (discussed below) in cyberspace will be. So the "faster/ cheaper/smaller" mantra hints at future developments, but it certainly does not predict them.

IT IS USEFUL TO DISTINGUISH AMONG DEVELOPMENTS IN TECHNOLOGY, PRODUCTS, AND SERVICES

In attempting to understand the continuing role of the information revolution and its potential differential effects on various countries, regions, and cultures of the world, it is nevertheless important to understand general technology trends and the types of products and services they will spawn. In this discussion, we find it useful to distinguish among developments in technology, products (both hardware and software), and services.[1] We view *technology* as the idea or intellectual property based on scientific principles that allows creation of a product that embodies it; for example, wireless communication standards and protocols per se are a technology. A *product* (such as a cellular telephone) may involve hardware or software, and embodies one or more technologies. *Services*, similarly, result from the application of technology, but in the form of capabilities offered to users, usually in a form resulting from storage, access, and manipulation of information. A website that helps you locate the nearest music store might be such a service. (But note that as the physical and cyber worlds become intertwined, so does the distinction between products [including software] and services [enabled by such software and hardware].)

SOME TECHNOLOGY DEVELOPMENTS CAN BE FORESEEN

It is widely believed that the exponential growth in computing power that has been seen for decades now will continue for at least another 10 to 15 years, reaching the limits of silicon technology by about 2015. That exponential growth has been referred to as "Moore's Law," an observation made originally in 1965 stating that the density of transistors on integrated circuits doubles about every 18 months.[2] That trend underlies many of the other developments that are expected.[3]

There will be a continuing convergence of voice and data communications, and another major jump in available bandwidth during the next two decades. These developments will be characterized in first-world economies by

- seamless data, voice, video sharing

- near-universal connectivity

- application convergence through the Internet Protocol (IP)

- widespread moderately wideband wireless

- optical, multiwave lines and switches, allowing bandwidths of many thousands of gigabits per second

- significant data storage density increases, to the point where terabyte stores become practical and accessible

- increasing synergies and interrelationships between silicon, bio-, and nanotechnologies, with some possible exploitation of quantum effects for computing.[4]

Machine translation among key natural languages is a long-sought goal. Its availability, for example, would allow the informational riches of the Web—predominantly in English today—to be accessed by persons whose only language is Arabic, Japanese, Chinese, or Spanish (for example). Predictions here are more difficult; the general machine translation problem is unlikely to be solved in the next 20 years, but "you can have any two of the following three desiderata: high quality, general purpose, fully automatic."[5] For many purposes and limited domains of discourse, this will be good enough for useful applications.

We emphasize in particular the importance of the very strong synergies developing between bio-, nano-, and material technologies. Beyond semiconductors, on-chip integration of logic and other components will include chemical sensors and components, electro-optical devices, and biological components as well as microelectromechanical systems (MEMS). The results, especially for sensor technology—and when combined with wireless communication developments—will be revolutionary, with an expected cornucopia of new devices and applications.[6]

PRODUCT DEVELOPMENTS WILL ALLOW INFORMATION DEVICES TO BE UBIQUITOUS, WEARABLE, AND IN CONTINUOUS CONTACT

Given developments in underlying computing and communication technologies, we expect to see a multitude of diverse, powerful, inexpensive sensors, and other devices capable of (limited-distance) wireless communication. Among them are tiny video cameras, MEMS microphones, accelerometers, gyros, Global Positioning System (GPS) receivers providing location and timing information, smell sensors, food spoilage sensors, biosensors, and polymer-based sensors. These products will provide a vastly increased coupling between the physical world and the cyber world, allowing information systems to react much more comprehensively to (changes in) their environment, and physical systems to react to changes in the cyber world while reacting to new information from elsewhere in the physical world.[7]

Computing and information systems will become much more ubiquitous, with convergence of wireless telephones, personal digital assistants (PDAs), radio, voice and email messaging, smart home appliances, etc. Precursor products in this trend are the Palm series of PDAs and Research In Motion's (RIM's) BlackBerry. Developments in such small, portable, personal devices, along with sensing technology, will make wearable computers increasingly important informational aids. Aiding in these developments will be protocols for short-range wireless communication, such as the IEEE 802.11 or Bluetooth standards or their successors.

Display products will undergo dramatic improvement within the coming 15 to 20 years. The above-mentioned synergies between bio-, nano-, and silicon technologies are expected to result in "electronic paper" displays that can be rolled or folded and perhaps contain wireless links to personal or other information systems, digital displays that retain their content without requiring power to continually refresh them, and large-screen, flat-panel displays that can be "tiled" to desired sizes.[8]

SERVICES DEVELOPMENTS WILL GREATLY EXTEND ACCESS TO, AND THE USEFULNESS OF, INFORMATION SYSTEMS

There is a major shift under way in business emphasis, from products to services. Increasingly, businesses see specific products as elements or components of a broader service that the firm provides to customers. Information technologies are central to this new business model.

Kiosks Can Provide Easy Access to Some Information Services

The coming availability of "good enough" machine translation of languages and speech recognition could allow *widespread deploy-*

ment of kiosks at which a question can be voiced, and the riches of the Internet used, to provide a spoken or displayed answer. Such a kiosk may be a small structure (either temporary or permanent) in a public place, housing a display screen and computational power similar to a personal computer, and linked to a telecommunication line. It may even be reasonable to imagine the kiosk containing a small satellite dish by which Internet and other informational services are accessed, and solar cells and auxiliary batteries by which it is powered as a self-sufficient informational platform. We foresee such kiosks having more importance in developing countries, where ownership of information system access products may remain limited.

Services available from such a kiosk might—at least initially—be tailored to certain specialized areas, such as farming, weather reports, market prices for agricultural products, and so on.[9] In that manner, the complexities of translation and voice recognition might be overcome within a limited domain of discourse. The advantages of such "kiosk" information services over traditional media (e.g., radio) could be the provision of on-demand information tailored to the needs of the individual, communication in terms of maps and pictures, and perhaps locally stored information relating to an individual user that can help tailor his or her interactions across a series of them in the manner that "Favorites" or "Bookmarks" tailor usage of a Web browser to one person's preferences.

Entertainment Will Be at the Leading Edge of Novel Information Services

As is increasingly the case, *entertainment* will likely lead the way in novel services, with business-to-business e-commerce as a strong second force. As these information utilities grow, they will become backbones supporting increased lifelong learning and specialized training. Among the products and services expected to play a large role are[10]

- multiperson computer-based games, with tens of thousands of people interacting online within an "environment" simultaneously

- Web-mediated physical activity, such as interactive games requiring strenuous physical responses

- ubiquitous webcameras providing entertainment, communication (improved interpersonal interaction at a distance), and intrusive surveillance

- interactions with people of different cultures, aided by translation programs

- the ability to view athletic events from almost any vantage point

- video glasses that place images directly before a viewer's eyes

- pornography (inevitably)

- music and movies on demand, any time, anywhere

- e-books.

Information Services Will Play an Increasing Role in Health Care and Telemedicine

Health care services will increasingly be influenced by "telemedicine," in which some or all of the services will be IT-mediated. The opportunity to access information and actual care from a vastly expanded set of providers will confront both patients and health care professionals with a bewildering array of choices. This in turn may generate new dynamic brokering services. Increased use of telemedicine is one of the factors likely to increase the gap between rich and poor societies (e.g., because high, reliable bandwidth is often required); however, it is not the dominant factor. Other factors tending toward an increase in health disparities include the continuing spread of infectious and noninfectious diseases in developing countries and inadequate health care capacities and spending, with AIDS, tuberculosis, malaria, and hepatitis remaining problematic, especially in Africa.[11] Some benefits from the information revolution will accrue to poorer countries—for example, from their improved access to information and training materials. Other health benefits from the information revolution will accrue from better (computationally intensive) modeling of the interactions of various molecules and their folding patterns, allowing the tailoring of drugs at the molecular level, and even tailoring to individuals. Access to such benefits, however, is likely to remain limited because of their expense as well as various policy hurdles—at least during the coming decade.[12]

Online Education Will Have Increasing, but Specialized, Effects

In *educational services*, the greatest impact of the continuing information revolution is likely to be in lifetime learning and specialized training. These areas are burdened with few regulatory constraints, and there is already keen competition among providers of such educational services. Other important changes will occur in postgraduate education, where online education will allow students to customize their degree programs, enjoying lectures from and consultations with professors at multiple universities.

University undergraduate studies and K–12 education are likely to be less affected over the next 15 to 20 years because of a variety of social, political, and other factors, but they may be dramatically affected somewhat later. Especially at the K–12 level, inertia, entrenched unions, unfamiliarity with and inability to use new technologies, the costs of acquiring equipment and building infrastructure, and (for public schools) political interference will all constitute serious barriers to adoption of new IT-based teaching techniques. K–12 education also has a significant social and emotional maturation component that cannot yet be provided by distance learning.[13]

Micropayment Schemes Will Emerge to Handle Small Online Payments

Payment schemes such as *micropayments* will be increasingly important in allowing e-commerce services to charge small amounts (less than the cost of processing a credit card payment) for small services performed, such as reading a document or downloading a small file. "Dynamic brokerage" services will provide a decentralized capability for matching highly specific customer requests for packages of services with suitable offers of these services from a wide range of suppliers. This requires creating a standard vocabulary for articulating requests for services and for describing services offered. The availability of micropayment services is likely to cause restructuring of some existing businesses, such as a move toward "pay per use" for downloading information, rather than reliance on subscriptions. These services may also expand commerce to many small entrepreneurs or individuals providing access to specialized information for pennies per transaction—perhaps the equivalent in the information sphere of eBay's expansion of commerce in an auction format to millions of individuals.

MARKETS WILL DECIDE WHAT POSSIBLE PRODUCTS AND SERVICES BECOME ACTUAL AND WIDESPREAD

Although technology's progress makes many products and services possible, markets ultimately decide which will become so widespread as to have an effect on societies and cultures around the world. Some important market criteria that can determine the widespread adoption of a product or service are

- ease of use
- backward compatibility
- perceived advantages from use
- low- or no-cost ownership
- affordability
- noncritical failures
- state of the economy (affecting disposable income)
- importance and criticality of adoption compared with viable alternatives
- dependence on market penetration for a successful business model
- dependence on critical mass of users.

But it is also important to realize that the various applications of IT can be treated as either private goods, which are left to the market, or as public goods. The United States tends to treat most applications of IT as private goods. Other nations (e.g., India) are treating IT not only as a private good but also as a public good. They are not leaving it to the market to determine what happens regarding IT developments and applications. These differing approaches can lead to tensions between countries or regions regarding intellectual property rights, which may slow the globalization of information technology. Observers in the United States or other Western countries should take some care to temper their assumption of reliance on the market with other societies' approaches and viewpoints. As a result of these differences in approach, other nations may use IT in different ways than does the United States.[14] Possible implications for the United States include markets that are less global than expected for informational goods and services.

The Emergence of "Killer Apps" Can Greatly Affect Markets and Create Markets

It is also useful to distinguish between the market for invention (e.g., through support of university research or research and development budgets within corporations) and that for innovation (e.g., from access to and availability of venture capital).[15] How IT-related products emerge from basic research, go through revolutionary change, become breakthrough products, or undergo gradual evolutionary change—or do not do so successfully—depends to a large extent on the market for invention, and for innovation, within a society:

- If a society has weak markets for both invention of new technology and for innovation of new products, it will tend to produce gradual evolutionary change.

- A society with a weak market for invention, but strong in innovation, can produce breakthrough products.

- A society with a strong market for invention, but weak in innovation, will likely produce basic research but no entrepreneurs.

- A society with strong markets in both invention and innovation can produce revolutionary change.[16]

The wild card in applications and services is what is known as a "killer application"—one that makes a new market because everyone views it as a "must have" product or service. Examples are the Visi-Calc spreadsheet that greatly stimulated purchase of Macintosh personal computers (followed by Lotus 123 that stimulated purchase of IBM-compatible PCs), and Napster and its "peer-to-peer" cousins that created explosive Internet sharing of MP3-formatted music files. It is difficult to predict where future killer apps will emerge, but massive online, simultaneous, coordinated game-playing by thousands or tens of thousands of participants is one possible candidate.

SOME TENSIONS ARISING FROM THESE DEVELOPMENTS WILL AFFECT THE GROWTH AND SPREAD OF IT-RELATED PRODUCTS AND SERVICES

A number of individual and societal tensions arise from the developments outlined above.

Optical Communication Technologies Are Highly Disruptive to Existing Telecommunication Industries Worldwide, and Other New Communications Developments Could Be as Well

It is increasingly clear that ultra-high-speed all-optical communication networks are a highly disruptive technology. It is likely that many present-day leaders in computer and communications industries will be threatened with extinction.[17,18]

The communication industry, especially in Europe, is also facing massive "3G" (third-generation) investment costs (for licensing and network infrastructure), yet the 3G wireless services promised have not yet sparked great consumer interest. At the same time, a grassroots "Wi-Fi" (wireless fidelity) revolution is taking shape in portions of the unlicensed spectrum, based on the IEEE 802.11b standard; this is threatening to undermine parts of the business plans of traditional telephone companies. Wi-Fi may be an enabler for a future "killer app."[19]

The possible rise to substantial use of IP-based telephony could be an additional disruptive influence.[20]

Open Source Versus Closed Source: Proprietary Standards Battles Will Continue

There are major battles to be waged between advocates of "open" versus "closed" worlds of protocols and standards. It is unclear where the balance will be found.[21]

Intellectual Property and Digital Rights Issues Are Creating Major Tensions

Among the many social tensions are increasing threats to intellectual property rights—for example, from new business models such as those exemplified by Napster and Gnutella. These issues are coming to a head with widespread sharing of songs in MP3 format and the likelihood of increased sharing of digital movies in MP4 format—both developments being fought with legislation and lawsuits by the Motion Picture Association of America and the Recording Industry Association of America. And it is likely that many of the new IT products and services will, as is often the case, primarily benefit those with the resources to obtain and exploit them. How these battles are fought (in courts, in legislatures, in the marketplace) and decided will not substantially affect underlying technology developments, but they will affect the types of products and services that each society or culture will have available.[22] The major tensions arising from these issues are likely to be between countries whose IT-based industries and services depend on enforcement of intellectual property rights, and other countries and regions not having comparable IT-based industries requiring protection.

A PERIOD OF INFORMATION TECHNOLOGY CONSOLIDATION IS BOTH LIKELY AND HEALTHY

The U.S. economy, in particular, has recently experienced a "dot-com crash" and is currently watching the implosion of the telecom industry. The events of September 11, 2001, created additional major disruptions in the U.S. economy, with some effects worldwide. There is a drastic reduction in the availability of easy venture capital money for the establishment of new IT-related companies. Tremendous amounts of slightly used, or even new, IT and telecom equipment are being auctioned off and sold from companies that failed, further depressing the market for new IT goods. All these factors compound, resulting in a period of slower growth of new companies and consolidation of existing ones. Given the frenetic nature of the "dot-com bubble," we regard these developments as healthy, overall, for the future development of IT technology, products, and services. During this consolidation, there are issues to be sorted out with some rational planning and decisionmaking: spectrum allocation for new

wireless products; potential fundamental restructuring of the telecom spectrum; "fair use" policies for intellectual property being
transmitted and used in cyberspace; patenting policies for software
and business practices encoded in software; the extent to which
Microsoft's operating system monopoly will be modified; standards
for security and various guaranteed levels of service on a next-
generation Internet; and so on. Working through these issues at
international, federal, and consortium levels will take some time but
can lead to a stronger foundation for substantial, yet sustainable, IT
growth in the coming decades.

NOTES

[1] A similar distinction, but one varying in some aspects—including the use of the term
"artifact" in place of "product"—was described in the proceedings of the first conference in this series. See Hundley et al. (2000), Section 10. This distinction also formed
the basis of much of the discussion within the second conference upon which much of
the discussion in this chapter is based. (See Anderson et al., 2000.)

[2] The original statement of Moore's Law had transistor density doubling every 12
months, but the pace has been a doubling every 18 months in the recent past, and that
is taken to be the form of the law now.

[3] See, for example, the International Technology Roadmap for Semiconductors (2001
edition) at http://public.itrs.net/Files/2001ITRS/Home.htm (accessed April 7, 2003).
An overview of the technologies contributing to higher-speed, smaller computing
chips is contained in a set of briefing charts accompanying a speech, "Beyond the
Wall: Technologies for the Future," by Karen H. Brown, National Institute of Standards
and Technology (February 26, 2001), given at the International Society for Optical
Engineering's (SPIE's) 2001 Symposium on Microlithography. The charts are available
at http://www.nist.gov/speeches/SPIE_022601.pdf (accessed April 7, 2003).

[4] See the Karen Brown charts cited in the previous endnote.

[5] This quotation is from Anderson et al. (2000), p. 11. The discussion at that conference
distinguished between "shallow" translation, between sentences of actual languages,
and "deep" translation, in which the source language is translated first to some
semantically explicit interlingual representation and from there to the target languages. The shallow approach tends to use dictionary lookup of words along with
some simple cues—and the results are of relatively low quality. The deep systems can
achieve higher quality but are more expensive and require a constrained domain of
discourse, such as a kiosk with travel information in a specific locale or translation of
training manuals for a specific company's products.

[6] See Antón, Silberglitt, and Schneider (2001). See also the brief discussion in the Science and Technology section of NIC (2000). We return to this subject in Chapter Fifteen.

[7]See Antón, Silberglitt, and Schneider (2001).

[8]See Mann (2001). Also available at http://www.technologyreview.com/articles/mann0301.asp (accessed April 7, 2003).

[9]Such kiosk-based information services would also be accessible through other devices such as home-based PCs, small portable wireless devices, etc. that have network access.

[10]These services will depend on access devices such as those mentioned earlier.

[11]See the section on Health in NIC (2000).

[12]For example, in the United States, health care policy has not yet made telemedicine a legitimate way to deliver even the most basic services.

[13]These views are based on a U.S. perspective; the situation may well differ in other nations.

[14]See the additional discussion of societal factors in adoption of technology in Chapter Six of this report.

[15]In this discussion, we distinguish between *invention* of technologies and *innovation* of products and services. This is, of course, an oversimplification.

[16]These statements are taken from Anderson et al. (2000), p. 55.

[17]This process is already well under way in the telecommunications industry. The reasons for the trend are documented in detail in issues of the subscription newsletter, *The Cook Report on the Internet* (Cook Network Consultants, 431 Greenway Ave., Ewing, NJ 08618). The basic argument is that optical, multiwave transmission lines and optical amplifiers and switches will make possible all-optical networks with a quantum jump in communications bandwidth, to thousands of gigabits per second. This trend, even in its early stages today, is creating a major glut of bandwidth, leading to a "race to the bottom" of firms trying to sell this capacity in order to recoup the investment. The bankruptcy of some existing telecom firms, and their strategy to undercut the pricing of others to gain some revenue, is only exacerbating the situation.

[18]In the computer industry, all-optical fiber and switching networks have not yet caused major disruptions, but they will. The transmission speeds that these networks will provide, thousands of gigabits per second, are greater than the main memory bus speeds of current workstations. This will give rise to major changes in computer architectures, operating systems, and networking protocols. Application software will also change, probably becoming much more distributed as communications capabilities expand and costs decrease dramatically. These changes, potentially as disruptive as the transition from mainframes to microcomputers in the 1970s and 1980s, will threaten present-day leaders in the computer industry with extinction. (See the white paper by David J. Farber, "Predicting the Unpredictable: Technology and Society," reprinted as Appendix A in Anderson et al., 2000.)

[19]See Stone (2002). Also available at http://www.businessweek.com/technology/content/apr2002/tc2002041_1823.htm (accessed April 7, 2003).

[20]See Cook Network Consultants (2003), especially pp. 15–37, for a discussion of IP-based telephony, often termed "Voice over Internet Protocol," or VoIP. Romero (2003) provides a briefer description of the current situation.

[21]See, for example, Edwards (2001). Also available at http://www.darwinmag.com/connect/opinion/comment.html?ID=375 (accessed April 7, 2003).

[22]A thoughtful analysis of intellectual property issues in the information age is contained in Lessig (2001).

THE INFORMATION REVOLUTION IS ENABLING NEW BUSINESS MODELS THAT ARE TRANSFORMING THE BUSINESS AND FINANCIAL WORLDS

The information revolution is enabling a variety of new business models that over the course of time are transforming the business and financial worlds.

MANY NEW BUSINESS MODELS ARE ARISING

Advances in IT are enabling a wide variety of new business models, for the internal organization and functioning of business enterprises and for their external interactions with customers, suppliers, and competitors. These models come in many different forms. Typical features include the following:[1]

- A much greater focus on the customer, becoming the dominant factor in business today, and on competition, fundamental to the development and progress of a business enterprise.[2]

- Competition dynamics that are often nonlinear, where small initial differences between competing products or services can lead to large divergences in final market position. (When this occurs, it is frequently a result of network externalities, including demand-side economies of scale and positive feedback.)[3]

- A customer service approach to developing everything, in which businesses are driven by information from the real, customer world, not the internal company world, and the entire product cycle (including development, production, marketing, and sales) is closely integrated and much more quickly responsive to market changes than hitherto, leading to what some have termed real-time, event-driven business enterprises.[4]

- Products and services customized for small groups of customers, and sometimes even for individual customers, with differential, value-based pricing (rather than the previous cost-based pricing).[5,6]

- Globalization, in all its manifestations, so that companies increasingly think of themselves as operating on a global stage, rather than a regional or national stage, regarding their suppliers and vendors, customers, and competitors, as well as the location of their design, development, production, marketing, and sales operations.[7]

- A redefinition of basic business functions, with new paradigms for products, services, delivery, support, and pricing.[8]

These new business models are transforming the business and financial worlds. Internally, they are changing the architectural organization of companies—often from vertical integration to horizontal networks. Externally, they are creating new modes of supply chain management and customer relationship management, coupling companies much more tightly to their suppliers and customers. Taken together, these internal and external changes are speeding up business information cycles and decision processes, rendering companies that undergo these changes much more responsive to changing competitive situations and customer needs, with products and services tailored to and differentiated for small groups of customers—and often even individual customers.

Electronic Commerce Is Becoming Increasingly Important

Many, if not most, of these new business models feature one form or another of electronic commerce, which is rising in importance as a major form of economic activity. E-commerce is bringing with it accompanying changes in the nature and structure of markets and the elimination of a wide variety of middlemen heretofore facilitating economic transitions.[9]

The initial stages of e-commerce adoption usually focus on cost reduction via increased efficiencies and effectiveness within existing business models. Later stages of e-commerce adoption frequently involve revolutionary changes in the business models, often initiated by new, entrepreneurial companies.[10]

E-commerce can be business-to-consumer (B2C) or business-to-business (B2B); B2B transactions at present far exceed B2C (including government-to-citizen) transactions. Today it is estimated that only 2 percent of global B2C and B2B transactions take place online, but this is projected by some to grow to almost 20 percent by 2005.[11] North America currently leads in the dollar volume of e-commerce transactions, with Europe and the Asia-Pacific region moving up rapidly and other parts of the world following along behind.[12]

An ever-increasing use of e-commerce is expected to be one of the dominant features of the information world.[13]

IT-Driven Changes Are Furthest Along in the Financial World

Financial markets have been going electronic for the past quarter-century. The birth of the Web has resulted in a dramatic increase in both the speed and the breadth of change. IT-driven changes have transformed the manner in which individual investors manage their finances, the business models used by financial intermediaries and other financial service organizations, and the organization and implementation of financial markets.[14]

This process, in which individual investors, financial intermediaries and service organizations, and financial markets are all going online, is continually reducing transaction costs and moving the current system toward a more efficient financial market. North America and Europe are furthest along in this process, with parts of the Asia-Pacific region following close behind.[15]

These IT-driven changes in the financial world include both dis-intermediation and re-intermediation: a reduction in the number of traditional intermediaries (dis-intermediation) and an emergence of new, more-efficient intermediaries with modified organizational and functional structures (re-intermediation).[16] Taken together, this dis-intermediation and re-intermediation are bringing about a profound transformation in the institutional structure of global financial markets, with consequences that will affect a wide range of business communities all over the world.

Much of This Leading-Edge, IT-Enabled Business Activity Is Concentrated in Geographic "Clusters"

As noted above, the later stages of e-commerce adoption often involve revolutionary changes in the business models. This requires skills in innovation and business change. Based on recent experience, such skills are more likely to be found in "clusters"—geographic concentrations of interconnected companies and institutions in a particular field—than spread more or less evenly throughout a nation.[17,18] The presence of such IT business clusters in nations around the world is becoming a common feature of the IT-transformed business and financial world.

"Creative Destruction" Is a Common Feature of These Business and Financial Transformations

A frequent accompaniment of these IT-driven changes in the business and financial world is "creative destruction"—the elimination of older and less-efficient products and services and their replacement with new, more-efficient ones. This creative destruction of old products and services is often, but not always, accompanied by the economic eclipse of the companies producing them.[19] This creative destruction process is playing a central role in the development and application of information technology in the U.S. business and financial community. Other regions of the world, however, may be able to shape their information revolution course in a different way, limiting the degree of creative destruction.[20]

Information Work and Information Workers Are Becoming Increasingly Important

Much has been written about the rise in "information work" and "information workers."[21] This is becoming an ever-increasing fraction of economic activity and the overall workforce in many nations, as their business and financial worlds undergo the transformations discussed here. Over time, this will free many businesses in "knowledge industries" to relocate to new areas more suited to information work than to manufacturing work, which in turn will affect where people live.[22]

This rise in information work will also affect the education required of people, both initially and over their careers. Regarding the latter (i.e., life-long learning), education today in the developed world is based on the assumption that what is learned in the first part of life will satisfy long-term knowledge needs. But the information revolution has made for much shorter knowledge life cycles than in the past, resulting in the need for continuous learning just to keep pace with the moving state of the art in most professional domains. Over time, this should have significant impact on educational establishments throughout much of the world.

This IT-Enabled Business and Financial Revolution Will Be Ongoing for Some Time

These IT-enabled changes in the business and financial world have been under way for some time, quickening in the past decade.[23] They are furthest along in North America, closely followed by Europe and parts of the Asia-Pacific region. But even in North America, and even more so in other parts of the world, much more is still to come. For the foreseeable future, an unending series of new IT developments will continually drive this ongoing revolution in the business and financial world, along both current and new paths.

Recent Developments May Temporarily Slow the Pace of These Transformations in the Business and Financial World and Affect Their Near-Term Character, but Not Their Ultimate Magnitude and Importance

The dot-com crash, which is largely over now, and the telecom implosion, which is still under way, have muted much of the hype that accompanied the information revolution a few years ago.[24] These two events have certainly slowed down the rate of investment in new IT-related businesses and, consequently, the pace of the transformations discussed above.[25]

However, if history is any guide, this slowdown is likely to be only temporary. Similar investment "bubbles" have been a feature of the early stages of other transformational technologies. Once each of these initial bubbles collapsed, a period of restrained activity ensued, followed, in almost all cases, by a resumption of growth in the new technology-driven industries along more stable and enduring directions.[26,27] We expect IT-related industries to follow this same path over the next one to two decades.[28]

The events of September 11, 2001, are another matter. These events could bring a heightened awareness of cyberspace security issues, as concern regarding future terrorist attacks expands beyond using hijacked aircraft as guided missiles to include a broader range of attack mechanisms and targets, including cyberspace-mediated attacks on business and financial targets.

This could lead to an increased emphasis on security considerations in the design, implementation, and operation of new IT systems serving the business community.[29] This would affect the near-term character of some IT-driven transformations in the business world but not the ultimate magnitude and importance of those transformations.

These Transformations in the Business and Financial World Are Changing the Playing Field for Governments and Societies

These IT-enabled changes in the business and financial world are in turn changing the underlying economic environment in which governments operate and societies function, thereby raising new governmental and societal challenges. We discuss these challenges, including the demands of "electronic government," or "e-government," in the next two chapters.

NOTES

[1] These new business models were discussed, in general terms, at the November 1999 RAND information revolution conference. (See Hundley et al., 2000, pp. 28–32.)

[2] In the relationship between firms and their customers, the information revolution has shifted the balance of power toward the customer. Consumers today can search the Internet for products, compare prices, and find review information. The Internet is being turned into what some economists would call a "perfect" competitive market, with ever-lower transaction costs for an ever-increasing number of products and services as time goes on. (See, for example, Fan et al., 2002, pp. 12–19.)

[3]With many information products and services, their value to each individual user is often proportional to the number of other users—so that their overall value is proportional to the square of the number of users (Metcalfe's Law). When this occurs, the greater the number of users, the greater the attraction of the product or service to additional users (demand-side economies of scale). This leads to a situation where products or services with a larger market share gain an even greater share and those with a smaller market share are driven to a still smaller share (positive feedback). (See Shapiro and Varian, 1999, particularly pp. 173–225, for a discussion of these and other economic features of the information economy.)

[4]Siegele (2002) describes the likely characteristics of such real-time, event-driven business enterprises, using material originally developed by Ranadivé (1999).

[5]Advances in IT make it possible for companies to maintain databases on the buying habits and preferences of individual customers. When this information is combined with modern, IT-enabled supply- and production-chain management systems, products and services can be tailored for small groups of those customers, and sometimes even for individual customers. Toffler (1970) introduced the term "mass customization" to describe this phenomenon, which he predicted would develop over time; NAS/CSTB (1994) describes its emergence in the early 1990s; and *BusinessWeek* (2002a) provides a look at the current state of this trend.

[6]Many if not most information products are costly to *produce* (the first time) but cheap to *reproduce*. Further, once the first copy of an information product has been produced, most costs are sunk and cannot be recovered. Economists would say that the production of information goods involves *high fixed costs* but *low marginal costs*. When the marginal costs for additional units are very low, if not near zero, cost-based pricing (based on those marginal costs) does not lead to a sustainable business model. Rather, value-based pricing, based on the value to the individual (or group) customer, is more appropriate. The key to achieving and maintaining such value-based pricing is product differentiation. Shapiro and Varian (1999, particularly pp. 19–51) discuss the pricing of information goods in some detail, including consideration of market structures for information goods, first-mover advantages (which do not always occur), and personalized and group pricing.

[7]Engardio, Bernstein, and Kripalani (2003) give a recent picture of how the outsourcing and "offshoring" associated with globalization are moving IT-related or enabled jobs around the world.

[8]Shapiro and Varian (1999) give a detailed discussion of these new paradigms for products, services, delivery, support, and pricing in the information economy.

[9]Symonds (1999) surveys the state of business to-business e-commerce around the world as of June 1999; Peet (2000) surveys the state of business-to-consumer e-commerce as of February 2000. Fan et al. (2002) focus on the impact of e-commerce on financial markets. Kraemer, Dedrick, and Dunkle (2002) survey how some 2,000 relatively technologically more advanced businesses in 10 countries—Brazil, China, Denmark, France, Germany, Japan, Mexico, Singapore, Taiwan, and the United States—are using e-commerce as of 2002.

[10]These stages of e-commerce were defined during the discussions at the November 1999 RAND information revolution conference. (See Hundley et al., 2000, p. 27.)

[11]Oakes (2002) gives the following projections for the percentage of business transacted electronically:

Region	2000	2001	2002	2003	2004	2005
North America	4%	6%	11%	14%	17%	20%
Europe	1%	2%	4%	7%	13%	20%
Asia Pacific	1%	2%	4%	7%	12%	18%
Latin America	1%	2%	4%	7%	12%	20%
Eastern Europe	0%	1%	2%	3%	6%	10%
Rest of world	0%	1%	1%	3%	5%	9%
Global e-commerce	**2%**	**3%**	**6%**	**9%**	**14%**	**19%**

[12]Oakes (2002) gives the following projections for the global volume of e-commerce in billions of dollars:

Region	2000	2001	2002	2003	2004	2005	5-year annual growth rate, 1999–2004
Global e-commerce	**1,231**	**2,251**	**4,363**	**6,581**	**9,852**	**14,191**	**63%**
North America	826	1,429	2,727	3,456	4,287	5,232	45%
Europe	178	372	760	1,479	2,662	4,298	89%
Asia Pacific	166	329	638	1,192	2,080	3,283	82%
Latin America	48	96	187	355	637	1,048	85%
Eastern Europe	7	15	29	56	103	182	90%
Rest of world	6	11	22	43	82	150	93%

[13]As Liebowitz (2002), especially pp. 58–95, has pointed out in his analysis of the economics of B2C e-commerce, this should work well for some but not all consumer products. He identifies the characteristics of consumer products that are likely to determine whether or not they can be sold profitably over the Internet and lists the types of products that should be most compatible with full-fledged e-commerce—which he calls e-retailing, or "e-tailing"—and those products likely to be poor candidates for sale over the Internet.

[14]Fan et al. (2002) discuss these IT-driven changes in the financial world in detail.

[15]This process is sensitive to public opinions or concerns that may exist in various countries (e.g., consumer confidence in IT-mediated financial transactions) and the closer connections between international markets and economies that exist today.

[16]The emergence of IT-driven dis-intermediation and re-intermediation are described in NAS/CSTB (1994). Their current state in the financial world are discussed in Fan et al. (2002, pp. 8–9).

[17]See Porter (1998) for a discussion of the dynamics of such clusters. Micklethwait and Wooldridge (2000), pp. 210–214, describe some of the characteristics of successful IT business clusters. Kotkin (2000) describes how they are changing the economic and social geography of the United States. Fairlamb and Edmondson (2000) identify a number of such clusters in Europe. Hillner (2000) identifies 46 such geographic clusters of IT activity around the world. She terms these geographic "hubs" rather than "business clusters," but the meaning is the same. UNDP (2001, p. 45) also contains a listing of Hillner's clusters, terming them "global hubs of technological innovation."

[18]This is not a new phenomenon. The industrial revolution started in similar clusters in England.

[19]See Schumpeter (1942), particularly pp. 81–86, for the original statement of the "creative destruction" thesis. Grove (1996) and Christensen (1997) present two of the most recent expositions of Schumpeterian creative destruction.

[20]Many Europeans are hoping to proceed in this fashion; only time will tell if this is a real possibility. (See the discussion in Hundley et al., 2001.)

[21]Peter Drucker was one of the first to write extensively regarding information work and information workers; he termed them "knowledge workers." (See, for example, Drucker 1989, 1993.) Reich (1991) postulated that three broad categories of work are emerging: routine production services, in-person services, and symbolic-analytic services. The latter category, constituting "information work," represents an ever-increasing fraction of the whole in many nations.

[22]This process is already well along in the United States, as predicted by Reich (1991) and described in Kotkin (2000).

[23]The recent dot-com crash and telecom implosion have slowed the pace of these changes somewhat in some sectors of the business and financial world. We view this as only a temporary phenomenon.

[24]*BusinessWeek* (2001) provides an overview of the dot-com crash; *The Economist* (2002b) describes the business and financial crisis in the global telecommunications industry in recent years.

[25]The monthly "Cash Flow" column in the magazine *Red Herring* tracks the rate of investment, by venture capitalists and others, in new IT-related businesses, both in the United States and around the world. The data presented in this column over time clearly show the marked drawdown in such investments since the venture capital investment peak in 2000.

[26]The railroad boom and bust in the 1870s is a classic example of this phenomenon. In the early 1870s, railroads drove economic expansion in the United States and created wealth much like telecom and Internet investment did in the 1990s. According to Davis (2002):

> Intercontinental railroads turned the U.S. into a unified market from coast to coast. Retailers expanded to supply immigrants building the tracks. Land values soared along the routes. Cargo that had taken weeks to travel by boat and wagon moved in days, a speed-up as revolutionary as the one that networked computers brought in the 1990s.

The railroad era was riddled with miscalculation and speculation, with the speculators growing rich—temporarily. In 1873, everything collapsed. Again according to Davis:

> An over extended railroad financier . . . declared bankruptcy, setting off a panic on Wall Street. The New York Stock Exchange closed for 10 days. A fifth of the railroads filed for bankruptcy. The stocks sank by a third between the end of 1873 and the middle of 1877.

But then things turned around. Returning to Davis:

> But then the railroads once again powered an expansion. . . . By 1880, technological gains, including mightier locomotives and better signal systems, were reducing shipping costs for manufacturers and department stores. The 1881 arrival of refrigerated rail cars helped create a national meatpacking industry. Montgomery Ward turned to railroads to deliver catalogs and fill orders. As demand surged, mothballed railroads came back into service, and more were built. Railroad stocks revived.

This resumption of growth in railroad-related industries proved to be stable and enduring, paving the way for several decades of U.S. economic growth. (See Davis, 2002, for a longer discussion of the 1870s railroad bubble, its collapse, and the subsequent resumption of long-term technology-driven growth.)

[27]Spar (2001) describes similar phases of early euphoria, a subsequent investment bust and industry consolidation, a period of restrained activity, and then the resumption of enduring growth, during the early stages of the telegraph, radio, and television industries.

[28]*BusinessWeek* (2001) provides a vision of how IT-related industries will recover from their current malaise and continue to transform the business and financial world—in its words, "unevenly and in stages."

[29]In response to market forces, up until now functionality has almost always been given much greater weight than security in the design of new IT systems and networks and their subsequent implementation and operation. This has led to a situation where security vulnerabilities are commonplace, security incidents are a frequent occurrence, and the business community—except for the financial services industry—has treated these incidents as a "cost of doing business." (PCIPB, 2002, gives an overview of the state of security, and insecurity, in cyberspace today, as well as an outline of the things that the business community, as well as other users of cyberspace [e.g., government, higher education, individual home users], need to do to secure cyberspace.)

THE INFORMATION REVOLUTION IS AFFECTING MECHANISMS OF GOVERNANCE AND EMPOWERING NEW POLITICAL ACTORS

The information age is reconfiguring some processes of governance, as well as changing both the character and distribution of political power.

SOME TRADITIONAL MECHANISMS OF GOVERNANCE ARE BECOMING PROBLEMATIC

Some traditional mechanisms of governance (e.g., taxation, regulation and licensing) are becoming increasingly problematic, as the information revolution allows action beyond the reach of national governments. For example:[1]

- E-commerce is making transaction taxes (e.g., sales taxes) more difficult to collect. This could over time lead to more reliance on other types of taxes.

- Regulations are often not keeping up with new business models, leading in some cases to unstable excesses, in others hindering the advance of IT-related activities.

- Regulation and licensing are becoming increasingly difficult when service providers are beyond national jurisdictions.

- Limits on offensive or dangerous information (e.g., pornography, hate literature, bombmaking instructions) are not always honored by others.

In these and other areas, governments that are particularly affected[2] will have to find new mechanisms of governance, or will have to create new, near-universal international control regimes.[3]

NEW GOVERNMENTAL MECHANISMS ARE BEING ENABLED

At the same time that some traditional mechanisms of government are facing challenge, the information revolution is also enabling new governmental mechanisms, generally falling under the heading of "e-government." In general, this usually implies the use of IT to improve and (eventually) transform

- the manner in which governments interact with their citizens and provide public services to those citizens
- the management of governments' supply chains
- the conduct of internal governmental processes.

The first of these is analogous to the use of IT in business to improve and transform customer relationship management; the second, to businesses' use of IT in supply chain management; the third, to the way in which businesses are using IT to speed up internal communications and process efficiency and even, in some cases, to change the architectural organization of companies.[4]

These three thrusts of e-government are analogous to those in business, but today, at least, the business world is far ahead in exploiting IT.[5,6] It remains to be seen how truly transforming IT will be for governments and how long the process will take,[7,8] particularly in the developing world.[9]

NEW POLITICAL ACTORS ARE BEING EMPOWERED

The distribution of political power is changing, as new nonstate actors are being empowered by the information revolution, in the business, social, and political realms, at the subnational, transnational, and supranational levels. These new political actors include transnational business organizations, sub- and transnational special affinity groups (ranging across the religious, ethnic, professional, criminal, etc., spectra), other nongovernmental organizations, and, unfortunately but most assuredly, terrorist organizations.[10]

This leads to various concerns: What will the role and authority of national governments be vis-à-vis these emerging nonstate actors? Will there be new allocations of power? Will power be shared in new and different ways? Who will be accountable in the future information age? Will more and more decisions affecting nation-states be made by actors not accountable to the citizens of those states?

Such concerns are just beginning to manifest themselves.[11] How they play out could affect the course of the information revolution.

At the same time that these new political actors are emerging, advances in IT are making new Internet-based modes of interaction possible between citizens and their elected representatives, between candidates and voters, and among citizens themselves (when discussing political issues). Some have suggested that this could over time change the dynamics of politics, much as the advent of television did in the 1950s and 1960s. Others, however, question the imminence of such a change in political dynamics, if not its ultimate extent. The jury is clearly still out on this issue.[12]

THE INFORMATION REVOLUTION COULD OVER TIME CHANGE THE ROLE OF THE NATION-STATE: THE JURY IS STILL OUT

The nation-state has been the dominant governmental organization in much of the world for the past 400 years. Some scholars suggest that as the information revolution increasingly allows action beyond the reach of national governments and empowers new political actors, the role of the nation-state could change. For example, one leading scholar postulates that a diffusion of governance activities may occur, away from the centrality of the nation-state, with some functions migrating to supranational or intergovernmental organizations, some devolving to local governmental units, and some migrating to private market and nonmarket organizations (at the subnational, national, and supranational levels).[13] Figure 4.1 illustrates the diffusion of governance this scholar has in mind.

RAND*MR1680-4.1*

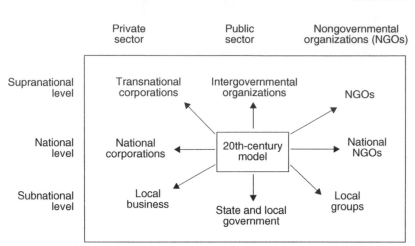

SOURCE: Modified from Nye (2002), p. 4.

Figure 4.1—The Diffusion of Governance in the 21st Century

One scholar has termed this the "retreat of the state."[14] Some scholars go even further, foreseeing the "end of the nation state."[15] But others feel that trends in this regard are by no means clear, pointing out the many essential functions that the nation-state will continue to play.[16] Considering these vastly different visions of the future presented by various "experts," one must conclude that for now the jury is still out regarding the future role of the nation-state in the information age.

Further, there are (at least) two different aspects of sovereignty:

- Constitutional sovereignty—the legal authority and primacy of national governments within their territorial domains.[17]

- Operational sovereignty—the ability of governments to exercise effective control within their territorial domains.

Constitutional sovereignty is not being challenged by the information revolution. But operational sovereignty is, both technically and with regard to cost.[18,19]

DIFFERENT NATIONS WILL TAKE DIFFERENT APPROACHES TO DEALING WITH THESE CHANGES

Governments will have to deal with these changes in mechanisms of governance (both positive and negative), with these new political actors, and with these emerging challenges to the traditional roles of the nation-state. Different nations may take different approaches.[20] How they do this will affect the future course of the information revolution in their regions and help define the role(s) of the nation-state in the information age. Smaller nations may more readily give up some prerogatives of the nation-state. Larger nations may be less willing to give up any prerogatives and may try harder to preserve the traditional roles of the nation-state. It is early regarding these issues; time will tell how this plays out.

In some cases, the paths that nations choose will adversely affect their relations with other nations, including, in some cases, even their closest allies. For example, in response to the many challenges confronting the nation-state in recent years, Europeans have willingly transferred many functions, responsibilities, and authorities traditionally within the purview of national governments to supranational organizations (most notably to the European Union but also to other supranational organizations). The United States has been much slower to move down this path. At least one observer believes that this differing approach may reflect a much deeper issue of principle regarding where the ultimate source of democratic legitimacy lies.[21] If he is correct, this could well lead the United States and Europe to define (and attempt to implement) greatly differing future roles for the nation-state—with continuing stress resulting for the U.S.-European relationship.[22]

THE EVENTS OF 9/11 MAY LEAD TO INCREASED GOVERNMENTAL INTERVENTION INTO IT DEVELOPMENTS

The events of September 11 should bring a heightened awareness of cyberspace security issues, as concern regarding future terrorist attacks expands beyond using hijacked aircraft as guided missiles to include a broader range of attack mechanisms, including cyberspace-mediated attacks on critical infrastructures.[23]

This may lead to increased governmental intervention into IT developments, to ensure that greater weight is given to security considerations in the design, implementation, and operation of IT systems and networks.[24]

NOTES

[1]These difficulties of governance in the information age were discussed in general terms at the November 1999 RAND information revolution conference (see Hundley et al., 2000) and are discussed in much more detail in Jones (2000).

[2]Some governments will be affected more than others. For example, those that rely heavily on transaction taxes, use regulations and licensing to closely control their business communities, or strictly limit pornography will have increasing problems over time. Those that practice a more laissez-faire style of governance in these (or other) areas will have fewer problems.

[3]Jones (2000) discusses the pros and cons of various new modes of governance that may prove feasible.

[4]These uses of IT in business are discussed in Chapter Three of this report.

[5]According to one authority on the status of e-government efforts in the United States (Mechling, 2002):

> The initial progress on e-government has followed a predictable pattern. As with most technologies in most settings, the early applications have been decidedly incremental. In essence, the Internet has been used to make services more convenient—available twenty-four hours a day from home and work and without time-consuming trips to government offices. So far, however, neither the Internet in particular nor computer networking in general has been used much for dramatic improvement in service efficiency, customization, and integration. In addition, we have made scant headway on concerns about the impact of e-government on privacy, security, equity, and the very legitimacy of our institutions of governance. The final success or failure of this trip remains very much yet to be determined.

[6]Even in the developed world, the transformative power of e-government is limited by the fact that government entities often cannot decide which customer segments to target—they have to serve everyone; and there are many other factors that differentiate governments' ability to exploit IT from the courses that private companies can pursue. (See Hundley et al., 2001, pp. 35–38.) In addition, *revolutionary* change is difficult to execute without creative destruction, and that is difficult to do in governments because they tend to be bureaucratic organizations.

[7]Mechling (2002) surveys how far federal, state, and local governmental agencies in the United States have come in using IT as an enabler to improve "bureaucratic government" and offers some thoughts on how IT might change the trajectory of government's evolution in the future. Picking up where Mechling left off in an earlier version of his paper, Donahue (1999) makes the following "five broad predictions" regarding the future evolution of e-government:

- For those governmental functions that are essentially similar to business functions, the information revolution will have essentially similar effects on cost, access, and innovation—but with a lag.
- Among the information revolution's most important impacts on government will be expanding opportunities for outsourcing.
- Wherever the information revolution improves potential *public* performance, it will also tend to ease privatization.
- The information revolution will tend to increase the productivity gap between public and private organizations.
- For those governmental functions that are essentially *dis*similar to business functions, the information revolution will have real but modest effects.

Generally speaking, these look like credible predictions, with one caveat regarding the last one: Even though warfighting is the governmental function probably most dissimilar to business functions, IT is already clearly having a major, transformational impact on warfare.

[8]The European Union has ambitious plans for e-government in Europe. The participants in the April 2001 RAND/NIC conference on the information revolution in Europe discussed the status of these plans and their prospects for success. (See Hundley et al., 2001, pp. 35–38.)

[9]PCIP (2002) provides a roadmap for e-government in the developing world, including 10 questions e-government leaders in developing nations should ask themselves before pursuing e-government, and details many of the obstacles that governments may encounter along the e-government path.

[10]International terrorist organizations such as al Qaeda are clearly empowered by their ability, for example, to carry out financial transactions and covert communications over the Internet.

[11]The demonstrations at international conferences over the past few years (e.g., recent World Trade Organization and Group of Seven meetings) may be one manifestation of such concerns. Arquilla and Ronfeldt (2001) discuss this issue.

[12]Applbaum (2002), Franda (2002), Hill and Hughes (1998), Kamarck (2002), King (2002), Norris (2002), Simon, Corrales, and Wolfensberger (2002), and Thompson (2002) present a sample of views on various aspects of this topic.

[13]See Nye (2002), pp. 3–5.

[14]Strange (1996) presents her vision of the "retreat of the state," or more precisely the "declining authority of states," as a result of the fact that "the territorial boundaries of states no longer coincide with the extent or the limits of political authority over economy and society."

[15]Ohmae (1995) presents the case for the "end of the nation state"—as a "meaningful aggregate in terms of which to think about, much less manage, economic activity."

[16]For example, Jones (2000) presents a detailed examination of the traditional purposes and forms of state action, the stresses that the information revolution and accompanying globalization are placing on them, the continued needs for governance

in a globalizing world, and alternative modes of governance to satisfy these needs. His conclusion: Although the information revolution and accompanying globalization do confront established states with serious challenges, the world will continue to need something like the nation-state to perform essential public governance functions.

[17]This is sometimes referred to this as "Westphalian sovereignty," in reference to the Treaty of Westphalia in 1648 at the conclusion of the Thirty Years War, which established the principle that nation-states do not interfere in the internal affairs of other nation-states.

[18]This point was made at the November 1999 RAND/NIC conference. (See Hundley et al., 2000, pp. 19–20.)

[19]It was also pointed out at the November 1999 RAND/NIC information revolution conference that this is not the first time national sovereignty has been called into question. Rather, national sovereignty has been viewed as challenged by each new communication media. See Hundley et al. (2000), p. 19.

[20]Jones (2000, particularly pp. 200–216) identifies a number of possible approaches that nations may take, including micro-, meso-, and macro-regionalism, various intergovernmental modes of public governance, and various mixed modes of public-private governance.

[21]According to Fukuyama (2002), which should be read in its entirety for a detailed exposition of this view:

> Americans tend not to see any source of democratic legitimacy higher than the constitutional democratic nation. To the extent that any international organization has legitimacy, it is because duly constituted democratic majorities have handed that legitimacy up to them in a negotiated, contractual process. Such legitimacy can be withdrawn at any time by the contracting parties. International law and organization have no existence independent of this type of voluntary agreement between sovereign nation-states.
>
> Europeans, by contrast, tend to believe that democratic legitimacy flows from the will of an international community much larger than any individual nation-state. This international community is not embodied concretely in a single, global democratic constitutional order. Yet it hands down legitimacy to existing international institutions, which are seen as partially embodying it.

The Economist (2002c, p. 24) has recently endorsed this view, saying:

> Americans, more than Europeans, see the nation as the ultimate repository of sovereignty and law. They may argue about the extent of federal powers. But Americans remain out of sympathy with European notions of international law or polled sovereignty. Indeed, their constitution forbids the transfer of Congress's sovereign powers.

[22]On this point, Fukuyama (2002) says:

> The U.S.-European rift that has emerged in 2002 is not just a transitory problem reflecting the style of the Bush administration or the world situation in the wake of Sept. 11. It is a reflection of differing views of the locus of democratic legitimacy within a broader Western civilization.

[23]The U.S. government has for some time been concerned regarding the cyberspace-related vulnerabilities of critical U.S. infrastructures. (See, for example, PCCIP, 1997). However, because most of these infrastructures are owned and operated by the private sector and therefore outside of direct government control, the government has thus far been unable to effect much of an improvement in their cyber security. (PCIPB, 2002, gives an assessment of the state of critical infrastructure cyber security today.)

[24]In response to market forces, up until now functionality has almost always been given much greater weight than security in the design of new IT systems and networks and their subsequent implementation and operation. This has led to a situation where security vulnerabilities are commonplace, security incidents are a frequent occurrence, and the business community—except for the financial services industry—has treated these incidents as a "cost of doing business." (See PCIPB, 2002, for an overview of the state of cyberspace security today.)

THE INFORMATION REVOLUTION BOTH SHAPES AND IS SHAPED BY SOCIAL AND CULTURAL VALUES IN SIGNIFICANT WAYS

THE INFORMATION REVOLUTION IS BEING ENABLED BY TECHNOLOGY BUT DRIVEN PRIMARILY BY NONTECHNICAL FACTORS, INCLUDING SOCIAL AND CULTURAL FACTORS

Outcomes of the information revolution are sometimes viewed as a product of how market forces on the one hand and government regulatory constraints on the other shape the deployment of technology-driven advance. But social and cultural values should be woven into the equation as well because they influence the course of the information revolution directly, as well as through their effects on both government policy and market activity.[1]

As evidence, note that many advanced democratic societies have access to the same information technologies. Yet they vary substantially in the extent of IT adoption, the nature of its use, and the apparent consequences. But the other direction of causation is also manifest. Globally networked information and communication media are already having profound effects on almost every aspect of society, and it is as yet unclear whether these will in general be forces for good (e.g., greater prosperity for all) or ill (e.g., unbridgeable social divides).[2]

In any case, social and cultural change will have to take place if individuals, organizations, and nations are to fully exploit the capabilities of IT—Schumpeter's concept of "creative destruction" was frequently invoked.[3] Yet human practices and the technologies on which they depend are situated in institutional realms (e.g., work, education, leisure) with embedded social norms, legal codes, shared histories, and the like. Institutional factors, however, are not easily changed and will limit the pace and scope of the information revolution. As one conference speaker put it, "Institutions change slowly. Internet time is fast. This disparity breeds tensions."[4]

Finally, the deployment of IT will inevitably produce unintended consequences. Such consequences, like the use of the Internet for communication among humans rather than for sharing remote machine resources,[5] are well known in the history of technological advance. These surprises result not from the technologies per se but rather from how humans use them. Moreover, the unintended consequences that arise when social and technical influences combine may well dominate the intended ones.[6] The bottom line, then, is that generalizations about the social and cultural dimensions of the information revolution are exceedingly difficult to formulate.

DIGITAL DIVIDES WITHIN AND BETWEEN NATIONS WILL PERSIST, BUT THEIR FUTURE SCOPE, DURATION, AND SIGNIFICANCE ARE SUBJECT TO DEBATE

Within countries, IT diffusion generally exacerbates disparities and reinforces social cleavages, at least until saturation has been achieved. For example, returns to education are increasing because of the growth of information work, widening the social gap between more- and less-educated workers. As another example, those who have connectivity can expand their social networks and can do so in location-independent ways, enabling them to take advantage of both strong and weak social ties.[7] Further, connectivity also may also enhance factionalism; that is, individuals with very narrowly defined interests can find like-minded others somewhere in the wired world. Moreover, the polarization between the advantaged and the poor is made more acute because of its visibility in the information society.[8]

By and large, the same sorts of growing and visible inequalities as a cause and a consequence of differential access to and use of IT are even sharper at the level of national states, as the discussion of regional variations below suggests. While there is reasonable consensus about the present existence of these digital divides, there is considerable debate over how their implications should be assessed. The European view, for example, is that digital inclusiveness is both a societal good and an economic asset; thus, a great many European Commission initiatives aim at producing equality of outcomes at the individual level and convergence at the national level. The prevailing American view is generally that policy should focus on establishing equality of opportunities, letting outcomes fall where they may.[9]

Whether or not these digital divides are regarded as problematic, and how severely so, is generally seen as a function of how much inequality can be managed and over what time periods. The prevailing American position is to downplay the consequences of the digital divide in the United States, taking the view that policy should focus on establishing equality of opportunities and let outcomes fall where they may. Further, Americans generally believe that the United States should aim at staying ahead of all other nations in the information revolution, rather than at converging on the same plane.[10]

ABILITY TO ACQUIRE AND USE KNOWLEDGE WILL BE CRITICAL FOR SUCCESS IN THE INFORMATION SOCIETY: DEVELOPING HUMAN CAPITAL APPROPRIATELY IS KEY

Knowledge work will constitute an increasing proportion of all work in the long-term future. This trend is already evident in the developed world; it will continue there and will emerge as well in less-developed parts of the world over time.[11] As a result, engendering, retaining, and nurturing intellectual resources—in particular, the sets of competencies related to production and use of knowledge—will be critical to global economic competitiveness. So "a quality education for all" will be one of the keys to a nation's success in the information age.[12]

Meeting the human capital challenge created by the information revolution presents different problems in different parts of the world. In the world's poorest countries, needs for basic literacy and numeracy skills stand alongside other basic societal needs (e.g., for adequate food, housing, and health services). Some developing areas and transitional economies, in addition to expanding basic skills in their labor pools, need to find ways to retain those with advanced competencies. Parts of Latin America, Eastern Europe, and South

Asia face the prospect of losing a significant proportion of their intellectual assets to Western Europe and North America, where knowledge work opportunities are growing and where the quality of life is higher.[13]

Nations in the vanguard of the information revolution face quite different sorts of challenges to human capital development for knowledge-based work. Most notably, the United States and parts of Western Europe are not producing an adequate supply of workforce entrants with high-level IT-relevant competencies in science, mathematics, engineering, and technology.[14] Presently these shortfalls are being remedied by in-migration from other parts of the world.[15] Another challenge has to do with providing for life-long learning. Education today in the developed world is based on the assumption that what is learned in the first part of life will satisfy long-term knowledge needs. But the information revolution has made for much shorter knowledge life cycles than in the past, resulting in the need for continuous learning just to keep pace with the moving state of the art in most professional domains.[16]

Advances in IT can play a role in resolving some, but not all, of these problems. For instance, globally networked information and communication systems may support "virtual migration," enabling workers with high-level IT-related competencies to fill labor force needs in the United States and Western Europe without having to leave their home countries.[17]

Similarly, distance learning technologies and programs can provide on-demand training and development to help employed professionals keep up with their changing knowledge requirements. However, many knowledgeable American and Western European observers believe the deepest problems have to do with the nature and content of their educational systems—problems that technology leaves untouched. One expert, for instance, called for revolutionizing education—refocusing learning institutions to support the continuous gathering and use of new knowledge in place of onetime acquisition and retention of stored knowledge.[18] But prospects for timely reform of long-established educational systems in advanced countries are not viewed as promising.

GLOBALIZATION, BOOSTED BY THE INFORMATION REVOLUTION, WILL CONTINUE TO HAVE MULTIVALENCED SOCIAL AND CULTURAL EFFECTS

Globalization is generally understood as referring to the expansion of networks of interdependence spanning national boundaries that follows the increasingly rapid movement of ideas, money, goods, services, and people across these borders.[19] While its economic effects are widely recognized, knowledgeable observers also gave considerable weight to its societal implications—both positive and negative. Among the main outgrowths of globalization, for instance, one expert recently cited the following:[20]

- erosion of censorship

- information overload

- democratization of information

- empowerment of individuals with information access.

That English is the prevailing language in all these phenomena tends further to widen the gap between political/intellectual/economic elites and others. And even among nations on the positive side of the digital divide, U.S. domination of the Internet in general and the Internet Corporation for Assigned Names and Numbers (ICANN) in particular is seen as a threat to shared and fair governance of an internationalized and interdependent information society.[21]

Further, the porosity of national borders to the flow of entertainment—especially from the United States—has additional impact. First, it fosters the globalization of styles (or at least fads), which leads those in some countries to feel that their own national cultures are being vitiated. Second, it makes the contrast between the rich and the poor all the more salient, potentially leading to polarization, unrest, hostility, and possibly a "clash of civilizations." Experts are uncertain about the long-term social and cultural outcomes of these trends.[22]

WILL IT-ENABLED GLOBALIZATION LEAD TO GREATER HOMOGENEITY OR GREATER HETEROGENEITY IN SOCIOCULTURAL TERMS? THE ANSWER IS "YES" TO BOTH

Shared norms, rights, and rules will be required for successful internetworking to conduct a range of political, economic, social, and cultural activities that span national boundaries. Developed countries will not be able to go their separate ways on major issues (e.g., intellectual property rights, privacy rights, freedom of expression) if they want fully to exploit the advantages of an internationalized information society.[23] Thus, the expectation is that a harmonized and stable infrastructure of laws and policies will emerge over time across national states.[24]

These shared frameworks are, however, expected to allow regional and local differences to flourish without becoming barriers to productive interaction. Moreover, individual creativity will be stimulated by the rich intellectual and cultural resources to which networked technologies give access. Further, protections for freedom of expression plus the capabilities afforded by interactive technologies allow individuals to produce, as well as consume, digital materials of their own choosing. Moreover, greater diversity is expected to be a benefit in a knowledge-based society, where there is little value added if everyone brings the same information and ability to the network.[25]

Thus, the information revolution will stimulate greater homogeneity in the institutional and legal infrastructures of networked societies while enhancing the heterogeneity of their constituent cultures.

THE INFORMATION REVOLUTION RAISES SIGNIFICANT SOCIAL-CULTURAL QUESTIONS FOR WHICH WELL-GROUNDED RESEARCH ANSWERS ARE UNAVAILABLE

What Is Effective Proximity?

Global networks are expected to facilitate location-independent choices of work, education, and leisure pursuits—choices that in the past would have required geographic proximity. However, it is not clear how well connectivity can support comparable levels of performance. For example, we do not know enough about the role of shared tacit knowledge and shared physical products in colocated interdependent work to understand how to create equally viable shared contexts via networked interactions—if this is possible at all (expert opinion is divided on this issue).[26] Similarly, the rise of high-tech clusters calls implicit attention to the potential role of geographic proximity in innovation and research and development creativity even when cluster members are at the forefront of the information revolution.[27] Finally, it is entirely possible that, in the absence of compelling positive experiences, localism may reassert itself over action at a distance.

What Are Viable Models for Leadership and Management in a Networked Global Society?

As social organizations, networks have distinctive properties. For example, group membership is partial, overlapping, permeable, and unstable; subgroups are not clearly delineated. Further, shared values rather than formal roles and structures are what link people. Finally, even at the global level, there is not a hierarchical system for action and decisionmaking; rather, leadership is negotiated among varied actors including national states, transnational corporations, and international nongovernmental bodies (e.g., World Trade Organization, International Monetary Fund, World Bank, World Intellectual Property Organization). While the Internet is sometimes offered as an example of distributed self-organizing collaboration, it is not clear how well its governance will hold up and in any case whether that model could be replicated.[28]

Can the Information Revolution Contribute Meaningfully and Measurably to Environmental Sustainability?

In Europe, in contrast to the United States, sustainability plays a big part in discussions of the future of the information revolution. It is hypothesized that the use of IT to reduce material consumption could make substantial contributions to environmental sustainability in the long run. Proponents of this view acknowledge that it would require structural changes in both lifestyles and business practices throughout the world; realization of these changes would demand the commitment of both civil society and the business community.

Others argue that opportunities to visit places virtually, to collaborate at a distance, and the like may well have the effect of increasing people's desires to travel and to communicate in person. Knowledgeable observers generally believe that at present there are very few data to support any inferences about relationships between the information revolution and sustainability.[29]

How Should Risk-Tolerance and Long-Term Planning Be Balanced over the Course of the Information Revolution to Yield Positive Social and Cultural Outcomes?

Societies and cultures differ considerably in their attitudes toward risk and social change. As noted earlier in this chapter, taking advantage of opportunities presented by advancing IT requires risk-taking and change. According to knowledgeable observers from both sides of the Atlantic, Europeans are more distrustful and risk-averse than Americans when facing social change; on the other hand, Europeans have a penchant for long-term planning that Americans do not share. But coping successfully on a societal level with the information revolution—whose end is nowhere in sight—will surely require a balanced mix of both. A major question, then, is how to engage flexibly in creative destruction. As one expert recently put it, "how can society continue coupling, decoupling and recoupling to generate innovative activity?"[30]

NOTES

[1]This conclusion from a plenary session in the first RAND information revolution conference (Hundley et al., 2000, p. 10) was echoed throughout the remaining conferences.

[2]See, for instance, Hundley et al. (2001), pp. 18, 25.

[3]See endnote 17 in Chapter Three and endnotes 29 and 30 in Chapter Six, as well as the discussions in Anderson et al. (2000) and Hundley et al. (2001).

[4]Anderson et al. (2000), p. 57. (See also Hundley et al., 2001, pp. xi, 19–20, 90.)

[5]This was the original purpose of the ARPANET, the predecessor to the Internet.

[6]Anderson et al. (2000), p. 57. For more discussion of the inevitability of intended consequences from reciprocal influences of social and technological factors, see Bikson and Everland (1998).

[7]Hundley et al. (2000), pp. 7–8; Anderson et al. (2000), p. 64; Hundley et al. (2001), p. 43; Treverton and Mizell (2001), p. 44. See also Fukuyama (1995); Anderson et al. (1995); and Bikson and Panis (1999).

[8]Hundley et al. (2000), p. 59; Hundley et al. (2001), p. 43.

[9]Hundley et al. (2000), p. 69; Hundley et al. (2001), pp. x, 5, 22.

[10]Hundley et al. (2000), pp. xii, 37–38; Treverton and Mizell (2001), pp. 44–45.

[11]Hundley et al. (2000), p. 9; Anderson et al. (2000), pp. 59–60. Levels of educational attainment are implicated, along with income levels, in the digital divides discussed above.

[12]Treverton and Mizell (2001), pp. xi, xvii–xix, 39–40; Hundley et al. (2001), pp. xv, 5. See also Enriquez (2001).

[13]Hundley et al. (2000), pp. 51–53, 71–72, 82–86; Treverton and Mizell (2001), pp. 40, 45–46. It should be noted, however, that improved conditions in the home country (e.g., economic growth, stable governance) would likely reduce the "brain drain" and might even induce a reverse diaspora, providing these regions with a wealth of human resources that could put them on a fast track to the information society. There is evidence of such trends in parts of India.

[14]Hundley et al. (2001), p. 68.

[15]A recent RAND report notes that both private- and public-sector organizations in the United States expect an even greater shortage of highly skilled entry-level IT professionals with degrees in science, mathematics, engineering, and technology if it becomes harder to employ foreign nationals (e.g., because of homeland security concerns). At present, a substantial proportion of U.S. academic degrees in these fields are earned by noncitizens (see Bikson et al., 2003).

[16]Hundley et al. (2001), pp. 5, 43.

[17]Anderson et al. (2000), pp. 63–64; Hundley et al., 2001, pp. 67–68. Some conference participants noted that virtual mobility permits employees to engage in rewarding knowledge work without the linguistic, familial, and cultural disruption that physical migration often entails. At the same time, it allows the employing country to avoid some of the strains associated with hosting immigrant populations.

[18]Anderson et al. (2000), pp. 68–70; Hundley et al. (2001), pp. 43, 89.

[19]See Bikson et al. (2003).

[20]See Hundley et al. (2000).

[21]Hundley et al. (2000), pp. 18–19, 35–37.

[22]Hundley et al. (2000), pp. xiii, 20–21, 36–39, 96; Hundley et al. (2001), pp. xvi, 96.

[23]As one participant in RAND's November 1999 information revolution conference remarked, "national-level laws do not make sense" in a global network. (See Hundley et al., 2000.)

[24]Hundley et al. (2000), pp. 67, 97; Hundley et al. (2001), pp. 22, 33.

[25]Anderson et al. (2000); Hundley et al. (2001), pp. 60–61, 86–87.

[26]Hundley et al. (2000), pp. 66, 98; Anderson et al. (2000), pp. 61–64; Hundley et al. (2001), pp. 20, 72. See also Bikson (2002).

[27]Hundley et al. (2000), p. 66; Hundley et al. (2001), p. 72.

[28]Hundley et al. (2001), pp. 32, 38.

[29]Hundley et al. (2001), pp. 29–33, 38–39, 69.

[30]Hundley et al. (2001), pp. 68–69, 90.

MANY FACTORS SHAPE AND CHARACTERIZE A NATION'S APPROACH TO THE INFORMATION REVOLUTION

Many factors shape and characterize a nation's or region's approach to the information revolution. Some of these factors are *causative;* they are the underlying factors shaping a nation's or region's IR posture. Other factors are *resultant;* they help characterize a nation's or region's IR posture, but are effects, not causes. Together these factors distinguish one nation or region from other nations or regions insofar as the information revolution is concerned.[1]

SOME FACTORS ARE CAUSATIVE

Rich Nations Are Better Positioned Than Poor Nations to Exploit the Information Revolution

As with much else in life, rich nations are better positioned than poor nations to take advantage of advances in information technology and meet the challenges posed by the information revolution. Rich nations—i.e., nations with high gross domestic product (GDP) per capita—are likely to have[2]

- well-developed physical infrastructures (e.g., electric power grids and telecommunications networks), providing a strong foundation for IT applications and IR developments[3,4]

- well-educated populations with high literacy rates, providing the human capital required to readily exploit IT advances

- strong financial and institutional support for research in information science and technology, leading to a ready supply of

> trained IT professionals and ready access to exploitable IT technologies

- legal structures permitting and enforcing rights to informational goods.

Poor nations—i.e., nations with low GDP per capita—are likely to be deficient in each of these areas.[5] This will impede their ability to exploit advances in information technology, thereby rendering it more difficult for them to meet the challenges posed by the information revolution.[6] Thus GDP per capita is probably the single most important determinant of a nation's IR posture.[7]

How a Society Deals with Change Is a Major Factor Shaping a Nation's IR Posture

The information revolution involves substantial change—in how people live and work, in how business is conducted and governance performed—ultimately affecting much of society. The manner in which a society deals with change is therefore another of the important factors shaping a nation's IR posture. There are two aspects to this:

- *A society's reaction to change.* Is it generally receptive to change or generally resistive to change? Does it see change as an opportunity or a threat?

- *A society's mechanisms for change.* Are these mechanisms predominately top-down or bottom-up?

There are many cultural factors, often rooted in history, that influence how a society reacts to change. Different combinations of factors can lead to similar end states. Resistance to change is frequently associated with a pronounced respect for authority, often found in strongly hierarchical societies. The predominant mechanisms for change in such societies are usually top-down.[8] Ready acceptance of change, on the other hand, is often associated with a comparative disregard for authority, more often found in nonhierarchical societies. Bottom-up mechanisms for change are more common in such societies.

The course of the information revolution in a society that is generally receptive to change and has many bottom-up mechanisms for change will be quite different from that in a society that is generally resistive to change and whose change mechanisms are primarily top-down. If nothing else, the information revolution should proceed much faster in the first society than in the second.[9,10]

Beyond such general cultural factors, there are a number of specific factors that affect a nation's ability to deal with change. These include the following:

- *Support or Compensation for Losers.* Change, especially major change in technology or economic organizations, generally produces winners and losers.[11] Often, the gains from change are spread thinly among the winners, while the losses are concentrated among a few losers who each lose a lot. The winners may not care enough or be well organized enough to lobby in favor of a generally beneficial technological change. But the losers have a lot at stake and often can find each other and organize to block technological change.

  Change will likely be easier in societies with good social safety nets, where provision is made for supporting or compensating those who are displaced by technological change.[12,13]

- *Labor Mobility.* Another characteristic that may be helpful in dealing with change is a high degree of mobility in the labor force. If a job disappears in one place, how easy is it for workers to pick up and move to another city where there may be opportunities?[14] This varies greatly from one society to another.[15]

- *Structure of Commercial Property Rights.* The structure of commercial property rights may have something to do with whether change is generally welcomed or not. What fraction of the population owns shares or is included in some form of profit sharing? Will many people benefit as a result of new technologies and their associated efficiencies? Or will these benefits be restricted to a narrow "owner" class?

- *The Consequences of Failure.* Almost inevitably, change involves risk. Willingness to run the risks of innovation or change will depend, at least in part, on the consequences of failure. In some societies, the legal, financial, and social consequences of failure can be very severe; in such societies the risk-taking spirit is, to say the least, dampened.[16] In other societies, business failure is condoned; in these societies, risk-taking is much easier.[17] Because much of the information revolution is being driven initially by changes in the business and financial world, the degree of risk-taking mentality in a nation's business and financial community will be particularly important.[18]

- *The Power of Blocking Interests.* What does it take to change things, to build things, to knock things down? Are property owners free to do pretty much whatever they please with their property? Or do they need approval from planning councils, workers councils, environmental regulators, city planners, labor unions, etc.? How strong are inherently conservative institutions—e.g., labor unions? Is the process for getting required approvals timely, transparent, noncorrupt, and generally predictable—that is, can you usually guess what the outcome of the process is likely to be—or is it a matter of chance every time?

Governments and Laws Can Be Helpful or Unhelpful

The degree and nature of the control that a government exercises over the various segments of a society is another important factor shaping a nation's IR posture. Government control can have both positive and negative effects insofar as a society's propensity to change is concerned, depending on the nature of the control. Nations with limited government control are, generally speaking, much freer to change than nations with considerable government control. However, there are historical cases where a strong degree of government control has led to significant societal change (e.g., Russia under Peter the Great in the early 1700s, Singapore under Lee Kuan Yew during the period 1965–1990, and China under Deng Xiaoping in the 1980s).[19]

The nature of the legal regime is also important. For the IT sector of a nation to flourish, a country needs good laws regarding intellectual property, a sensible approach to contract law and a strong willingness to enforce contracts, and a smoothly working system for handling bankruptcy so that the inevitable business failures that go with any rapidly changing technology can be managed. Also important, one would think, should be strong protections for freedom of expression.

The Structure of Capital Markets Is Also Important

The varying structures of capital markets in different nations represent another important differential determinant of the future course of the information revolution in those nations.[20] The availability of funding for new IT businesses and concepts and the manner of the funding process (i.e., the vagaries of getting funding, listings, capital, acquisitions, etc.) directly affect the growth and development of new IT industries in any given nation. This can be critical because new IT concepts and businesses are often antiestablishment by their very nature—they upset and challenge the old business models, monopolies, and ways of doing things—and yet money is a very establishment thing in most countries. The free and open flow of capital, the existence of seed and venture capital, and vibrant over-the-counter markets similar to NASDAQ (which give venture capitalists and startup employees an exit market) are critical enabling factors for the growth and proliferation of IT.

The ability of startups to get such funding differs greatly from one nation to another. Some nations aggressively use equity financing for startups. Other nations lack a strong equity culture and a secondary market, and rely much more heavily on debt financing. But debt financing requires a track record and punishes failure—both of which can be detrimental to startups.

These Causative Factors Can Play Out in Various Ways

These causative factors can play out in many different ways;[21] there are a large number of different possible combinations and many ways in which formulas can be devised attempting to predict a nation's performance in the information revolution.[22] In one of the more notable of these attempts, the United Nations Development Programme has recently created a "technology achievement index" as a "new measure of countries' ability to participate in the network age." This index focuses on four factors—creation of technology, diffusion of recent developments, diffusion of old developments, and human skills—and classifies nations into four categories: leaders, potential leaders, dynamic adopters, and marginalized.[23]

OTHER FACTORS ARE EFFECTS, NOT CAUSES

These factors add richness to the description of a nation's IR posture and serve as ways of tracking its IR performance.

The Degree and Nature of IT Penetration into a Society and the Distribution of Its IT Activity Across the Technology, Product, and Service Spectrum Are Useful Descriptors of a Nation's IR Posture

The degree and nature of IT penetration into a society is obviously one of the key resultant factors characterizing a nation's IR posture and tracking its performance. There are many ways of describing this penetration, emphasizing different aspects of IT penetration, which includes both consumption (i.e., use) and production of IT-related items.[24]

In further characterizing the IT activity of a nation, beyond mere penetration rates, some have found it useful to distinguish among[25]

- the underlying *technology*
- hardware and software *products* developed from that technology
- *services* performed and delivered using those products.

All nations are not equally strong and active in all three of these areas. Some are very active in IT technology development. Others are active in IT (hardware or software) product development but rely on other nations to develop the underlying technology. Still others are very active in the performance and delivery of IT-enabled services but rely on other nations for both the underlying technology and the products. The pattern of distribution of a nation's IT activity across this technology, product, service spectrum is another useful descriptor of its IR posture.[26]

Measures of Information Work and Workers and of E-Commerce Are Also Important Descriptors

Much has been written about the rise in "information work" and "information workers," as an ever-increasing fraction of economic activity and the overall workforce in many nations.[27] The amount of information work and information workers in a nation is another important descriptor of its IR posture.

Much has also been written about the rise of electronic commerce as a major form of economic activity.[28] *Stage one* of e-commerce adoption usually focuses on cost reduction via increased efficiencies and effectiveness within existing business models. *Stage two* of e-commerce adoption involves revolutionary changes in the business models, often initiated by new, entrepreneurial companies.[29] E-commerce can be business-to-consumer (B2C) or business-to-business (B2B). The amount of e-commerce in a nation, measured (for example) as a portion of GDP, and its general nature (e.g., distribution between stages one and two, distribution between B2C and B2B) are other important descriptors of its IR posture.

The Presence and Number of IT Business Clusters Are Important Descriptors of the Vigor of a Nation's IR Posture

As noted above, stage two of e-commerce adoption involves revolutionary changes in the business models. This requires skills in innovation and business change. Based on recent experience, such skills are more likely to be found in "clusters"—geographic concentrations of interconnected companies and institutions in a particular field—than spread more or less evenly throughout a nation.[30,31] The presence and number of such IT business clusters in a nation are still other important descriptors of the vigor of its IR posture, particularly in the business and financial realm.[32]

The Amount of "Creative Destruction" Going On in a Nation Can Be an Important Descriptor of Its IR Posture

As Joseph Schumpeter originally postulated and others have elaborated, an essential accompaniment of major innovation in capitalistic societies is "creative destruction"—the perpetual cycle of destroying the old and less-efficient product or service and replacing it with new, more-efficient ones.[33] This creative destruction of old products and services is often, but not always, accompanied by the economic eclipse of the companies producing them. This process has played a central role in the development and application of information technology over the past few decades, so that the amount of such creative destruction occurring in a nation, particularly in its technology, business, and financial arenas, is another important descriptor of its IR posture.[34]

The Presence of New Political Actors and Changes in Governance Are Measures of IR-Induced Change in the Political Arena

The distribution of political power is changing throughout the world, as new nonstate actors are being empowered by the information revolution, in the business and social arenas as well as in the political realms itself, at the subnational, transnational, and supranational levels. Where this process is taking the world is unclear. Some say it portends changes in the role of the nation-state.[35] Others are not so sure.[36] Whichever view turns out to be correct, the presence of such new political actors in a nation, and their number, may be one measure of the degree to which change is occurring in its political arena.

Also, traditional mechanisms of governance (e.g., taxation, regulation and licensing) are becoming increasingly problematic, as the information revolution allows action beyond the reach of national and subnational governments.[37] At the same time, IT advances are enabling new mechanisms of governance, new modes for delivery of governmental services, new ways for governments to interact with citizens, etc.[38] Again, where these processes are headed is unclear. Nevertheless, another useful measure of change in a nation's political arena could be the degree to which the role and manner of governance has changed in response to such new pressures and opportunities.

The Movement of Talented, IT-Trained People Can Be a Useful Indicator of a Nation's IR Posture

The process of globalization has not only removed barriers to the movement of capital but to the movement of people as well, particularly talented, IT-trained people.[39,40] Such talented individuals—information technologists, software experts, those with a creative mind and an entrepreneurial bent, etc.—are in increasingly short supply in all of the major geographical centers of IR development throughout the world.[41] Other nations (e.g., India), somewhat out of the IR mainstream, have a plentiful supply of talented, IT-trained people but fewer indigenous opportunities in the new economy.[42] In response to this supply-demand imbalance, the movement of talented IT professionals between nations has been growing throughout the world: into some countries, not into other countries, and out of some countries. Accordingly, a nation's balance sheet insofar as this talent flow is concerned is another useful indicator of its IR posture.[43]

NOTES

[1] In much of what follows, we will speak in terms of "nations." However, most of what we say can also apply to regions both larger and smaller than nations.

[2] GDP per capita as a measure needs to be balanced by considerations of distribution. Countries with a reasonably high GDP per capita attained by virtue of the fact that a very small fraction of the population are extremely wealthy while the vast proportion are quite poor, will not fare well (e.g., because they will not have well-educated populations with high literacy rates and a supply of well-trained IT professionals, let alone an abundance of people with access to electric power grids). So an extreme variance of the GDP measure across a nation's population will limit its usefulness as a determinant of a nation's IR posture.

[3] As Bill Gates (among others) has pointed out, before one can cross the digital divide, one must cross the electricity divide. (See Verhovek, 2000.) According to UNDP (2001, p. 42), some 2 billion people, a third of the world's population, still do not have access to dependable supplies of electricity.

[4] A well-developed telecommunications network is indeed an asset, but it also imposes legacy costs that in many countries inhibit rapid change.

[5] The annual human development reports of the United Nations Development Programme provide copious statistics on all these items and many other relevant ones, for both rich and poor nations all over the world. See, for example, UNDP (2001).

[6]Difficult, but not impossible, as UNDP (2001, p. 1) asserts, stating: "The technology divide does not have to follow the income divide. Throughout history, technology has been a powerful tool for human development and poverty reduction."

[7]GDP per capita may be the most important determinant, but it is not the only determinant, as the remainder of this chapter will indicate—as do the cases of China and India, two nations with relatively low GDP per capita that are emerging as important IT users and producers (see Chapter Nine of this report and Hachigian and Wu, 2003).

[8]If the central leadership in such a society has sufficient authority to overcome societal resistance to change, significant top-down-driven change can be brought about. If the central authority is weak, however, top-down-driven change may be slow in coming. China is an example of the former case, Japan the latter. (Private communication, William Overholt, RAND.)

[9]All segments of a society may not be uniform in their acceptance of change. Some may be more receptive, some more resistive. Some may have many bottom-up mechanisms for change. Others may have primarily top-down mechanisms.

[10]Given the obvious importance of cultural factors in influencing a society's propensity to accept change, the literature on this subject is surprisingly thin. Lipset (1996) has looked at the American propensity for entrepreneurship and innovation from a comparative cultural perspective. There is also literature regarding cultural barriers to innovation in Japan. But beyond this, there does not appear to be any book or study dealing with the question systematically. (There are books dealing with other aspects of cultural influences on national behavior—for example, Fukuyama [1995], Harrison and Huntington [2000], and Throsby [2001]—but none dealing specifically with the way in which culture affects how a society deals with change.)

[11]What we usually call technological progress usually produces more winners than losers; that is why we call it "progress."

[12]These provisions could take the form of retraining programs, generous unemployment insurance, help in finding new jobs, portability of employment benefits, etc.

[13]It is possible for the social safety nets to be too good, however, so that displaced workers feel no need to find new jobs but remain on the dole for lengthy periods of time.

[14]A number of factors feed into labor mobility. Culture and tradition are important, of course. Size of the society and linguistic and cultural homogeneity also play a role. How far can you move without going to a distinctly different culture? Also significant can be the character of residential property rights. Can you sell your claim to one residence and buy a claim to a new one? Family structure and family employment patterns matter too. Do you have to find just one new job in a new city, or do multiple members of a family have to find employment?

[15]Europeans, for example, are notoriously immobile. Not only are they reluctant to move from one European Union country to another (understandable because of language and cultural differences), but they often resist moving within a nation to take a new job. American workers, in contrast, are much more mobile.

[16]Until very recently, for example, bankruptcy in Japan was pretty much the "kiss of death." Bankrupts felt shamed and ostracized. If your business failed, you had very little chance of attracting financing for a new venture, and you would probably have a hard time finding another job.

[17]The United States is one such society. Business bankruptcy is no longer seen as a moral failing in the United States. Even if an earlier enterprise failed, entrepreneurs are able to attract financing for plausible new ventures. Bankruptcy laws provide effective protection from creditors.

[18]As Joseph Schumpeter (1934) originally showed and others have elaborated—see, for example, Scherer (1984) and Shionoya and Perlman (1994)—individual (or, less likely, organizational) entrepreneurs taking risks in the expectation of financial rewards are the driving force behind most innovative changes in the business and financial world. Therefore, the more risk-takers and entrepreneurs there are in a nation's business and financial community, the faster the information revolution will progress in that nation.

[19]In each of these cases, a strong, authoritative leader forced modernizing change on his people: Peter the Great, to bring about the adoption of Western European ways in Russia; Lee Kuan Yew, to move Singapore, in his words, "from the Third World to the First"; and Deng Xiaoping, to introduce market forces into the Chinese economy. (See, for example, Lee, 2000.)

[20]These remarks are based on discussions during the November 1999 RAND information revolution conference. (See Hundley et al., 2000.)

[21]This listing is intended to cover the major causative factors that will shape a nation's or region's IR posture, but it is not intended to be exhaustive; other factors could also help or hinder the information revolution in a specific nation or region.

[22]During RAND's November 1999 information revolution conference, four groups of factors were identified as being drivers of or impediments of change in the poorer nations of the world: *culture, competence, capital,* and *control,* termed the "four Cs." Hundley et al. (2000, pp. 84–87) describes what is included in each of these four factors. These factors were discussed at the 2001 NIC/State Department conference on information technology in Africa (see NIC/State Department, 2002, pp. 10–11) and are referred to in Chapter Twelve of this report in discussing the information revolution in Africa.

[23]For a full description of the UNDP Technology Achievement Index and a tabulation of the initial results for 72 nations from all over the world, see UNDP (2001, pp. 46–63, 246).

[24]For example, Wolcott (1999), focusing on Internet penetration rather than on IT penetration construed more broadly, uses six factors to describe this penetration:

- *Pervasiveness.* What fraction of a nation's population uses the Internet?
- *Geographic dispersion.* How widespread geographically is Internet usage in a nation?

- *Sectoral absorption.* How many different sectors of a nation's society and economy use the Internet?

- *Connectivity infrastructure.* How robust is the physical infrastructure supporting Internet connectivity in a nation?

- *Organizational infrastructure.* How robust is the Internet Service Provider (ISP) market supporting Internet access in a nation?

- *Sophistication of use.* How sophisticated are the uses of the Internet in a nation?

Other authors use varying measures. For example, Larry Press ("Worldwide Information Revolution Demographics," paper presented at the November 1999 RAND/NIC conference) expresses IT penetration primarily in terms of the fraction of the population that has access to the Internet or uses a personal computer. Wolcott et al. (1997) express a country's IT capabilities—which are related to but not congruent with the degree of IT or Internet penetration—in terms of five factors: proximity to the technological frontier, depth of development, sophistication of use, pervasiveness, and indigenization. UNDP (2001, pp. 60–63) presents IT-related data on 162 nations that can be used to support the application of each of these approaches. OECD (2002) presents various measures of the "information economy" in a number of nations (mostly, but not entirely, European).

[25]Here we view *technology* as the idea or intellectual property behind a product that embodies it, such as wireless communication technology per se. A *product* is an entity involving hardware and/or software (such as a cellular telephone or a word processing program) embodying one or more technologies. *Services,* similarly, result from the application of technology but in the form of capabilities offered to users, usually in a form resulting from storage, access, and manipulation of information. A website that helps one locate the nearest music store might be such a service.

[26]See Hundley et al. (2000) and Anderson et al. (2000) for further elaboration on the technology, product, and service construct—termed there the "technology, artifact, and service" construct.

[27]Peter Drucker was one of the first to write extensively regarding information work and information workers; he termed them "knowledge workers." (See, for example, Drucker 1989, 1993.) Reich (1991) postulated that three broad categories of work are emerging: routine production services, in-person services, and symbolic-analytic services. The latter category, constituting "information work," represents an ever-increasing fraction of the whole in many nations.

[28]Peet (2000) surveys the state of e-commerce as of February 2000. Fan et al. (2002) focus on the impact of e-commerce on financial markets.

[29]These two stages of e-commerce were defined during discussions at the November 1999 RAND information revolution conference. (See Hundley et al., 2000, p. 27.)

[30]See Porter (1998) for a discussion of the dynamics of such clusters. Kotkin (2000) describes how they are changing the economic and social geography of the United States. Fairlamb and Edmondson (2000) identify a number of such clusters in Europe. Micklethwait and Wooldridge (2000), pp. 210–214, describe some of the characteristics of successful IT business clusters.

[31]This is not a new phenomenon. The industrial revolution started in similar clusters in England.

[32]Hillner (2000) identifies 46 such geographic clusters of IT activity around the world. She terms these geographic "hubs" rather than "business clusters," but the meaning is the same. UNDP (2001, p. 45) also contains a listing of Hillner's clusters, terming them "global hubs of technological innovation."

[33]See Schumpeter (1942), particularly pp. 81–86, for the original statement of the "creative destruction" thesis. Grove (1996) and Christensen (1997) present two of the most recent expositions of Schumpeterian creative destruction.

[34]While the Schumpeterian creative destruction process has played a central role in the development and application of information technology in the United States over the past few decades, other regions of the world may be able to shape their information revolution course in a different way, avoiding some degree of creative destruction. (Many Europeans are hoping to proceed in this fashion; see the discussion in Hundley et al., 2001.) Only time will tell if this is a real possibility.

[35]See, for example, Ohmae (1995) and Strange (1996) for presentations of this viewpoint.

[36]See Jones (2000) for a presentation of the opposing viewpoint: that the nation-state will continue much as it is today.

[37]This phenomenon is also highlighted in the proceedings of the November 1999 RAND information revolution conference (Hundley et al., 2000).

[38]RAND's 2001 conference on the information revolution in Europe included a considerable discussion of "e-government," the use of IT to change (and modernize) the mechanisms of governance. (See Hundley et al., 2002, pp. 35–43.) Kamarck and Nye (2002) present a number of additional views of democratic governance in the information age.

[39]In many if not most cases, talented IT professionals are drawn to one or another of the IT business clusters discussed previously. Nations that have vigorous IT clusters attract IT professionals from other nations; nations that do not have such clusters do not.

[40]Both Friedman (1999) and Micklethwait and Wooldridge (2000) discuss this movement of talented, IT-trained people in general terms, as one of the ongoing features of globalization. NIC (2001) discusses global migration trends more broadly, including the movement of high-tech professionals. ACM (2001) devotes an entire issue to the global IT workforce, including its movement between nations.

[41]U.S. IT companies have been complaining about a shortage of trained IT professionals for many years. (See, for example, Shiver, 2000.) Recently, German companies have joined the chorus as well. (See Meyer-Larsen, 2000, for a discussion of this and other aspects of the current German business climate.)

[42]Sender (2000) describes the "brain drain" of Indian IT professionals out of India into the United States.

[43]For some nations, data on this talent flow are readily available; for others, obtaining them is difficult. For the United States, the inward flow of IT (and other high-tech) professionals is tracked by the H1B visa program, which in the late 1990s was running at a level of more than 100,000 high-tech immigrants per year, and which increased to roughly 200,000 in 2001. *The Los Angeles Times* ("Where the U.S. Is Getting High-Tech Help," 2000) presents data on the countries of origin of these immigrants in 1999.

PART II. REGIONAL VARIATIONS

Chapter Seven

NORTH AMERICA WILL CONTINUE IN THE VANGUARD OF THE INFORMATION REVOLUTION

For the foreseeable future, North America (i.e., the United States and Canada)[1] will continue in the vanguard of the information revolution.

THE NORTH AMERICAN ECONOMY AND SOCIETY ARE WELL POSITIONED TO MEET THE CHALLENGES OF THE INFORMATION REVOLUTION

The economies and societies of the United States and Canada are quite favorably positioned to do well in the information age because of the following:[2]

- They have well-developed physical infrastructures (electricity, telecommunications, etc.), well-educated populations, a ready supply of trained IT professionals, and ready access to exploitable IT technologies.

- Their economies and societies are generally receptive to change, adept at dealing with the consequences of change, and supportive of risk-taking, with deeply rooted entrepreneurial cultures.

- They have generally market-responsive governments, at all levels, that provide a basic environment hospitable to IT (and other) business developments and then (mostly) stay out of the way.

- They have legal regimes with good intellectual property protections, well-established contract and bankruptcy laws well suited for handling the inevitable business failures that go with any rapidly changing technology, and strong protections for freedom

71

of expression—all of which allow the North American IT sector to flourish.

- They have innovative and efficient capital markets with well-developed venture capital communities, well attuned to the funding requirements of new IT businesses and concepts.

- They are both nations of immigrants that attract energetic, talented, IT-trained people from all over the world.

These characteristics have placed the United States and Canada in an advantageous position, able to respond well to the challenges posed by the information revolution.[3,4]

NORTH AMERICA WILL EXPLOIT THESE ADVANTAGES TO CONTINUE IN THE VANGUARD OF THE INFORMATION REVOLUTION

Over the past few decades, the United States and Canada have exploited these advantages to assume leading, pathbreaking roles in most aspects of the information revolution.[5] Over the next 10 years, these nations should continue in the vanguard of the information revolution, taking leading positions in the development of

- new information-related technologies and devices, going well beyond what exists today[6]

- new products and services enabled by these IT advances, including new "killer applications"[7]

- new business models, further transforming the business and financial worlds.[8]

Selected nations outside North America—particularly in Europe and Asia—will be in the vanguard as well, with leading positions in some aspects of the information revolution, for some periods of time. But North America will be in the vanguard in most aspects of the information revolution, most of the time.[9]

"Creative destruction" will continue to accompany these developments, along with persistent increases in the role of electronic commerce, information work and information workers in the North American economy, and the continued formation of IT-business clusters in many parts of North America.[10] Also, the North American entertainment industry will continue its leading market position throughout much of the world.

THE DOT-COM CRASH AND TELECOM IMPLOSION MAY SLOW THE PACE OF IT-RELATED DEVELOPMENTS IN NORTH AMERICA, BUT ONLY TEMPORARILY

The dot-com crash, which is largely over now, and the telecom implosion, which is still under way, have muted much of the hype that accompanied the information revolution a few years ago.[11] These two events have certainly slowed down the rate of investment in new IT-related businesses in North America and, consequently, the pace of the IT-related developments discussed above.[12]

However, if history is any guide, this slowdown is likely to be only temporary. Similar investment "bubbles" have been a feature of the early stages of other transformational technologies. Once each of these initial bubbles collapsed, a period of restrained activity ensued, followed, in almost all cases, by a resumption of growth in the new technology-driven industries, along more stable and enduring directions.[13] We expect IT-related industries in North America to follow this same path over the next one to two decades.[14]

THE EVENTS OF 9/11 MAY LEAD TO INCREASED GOVERNMENTAL INTERVENTION IN IT DEVELOPMENTS IN NORTH AMERICA

The events of September 11, 2001, are another matter. The results of these events could bring a heightened awareness of cyberspace security issues, as concern regarding future terrorist attacks expands beyond using hijacked aircraft as guided missiles to include a broader range of attack mechanisms and targets, including cyberspace-mediated attacks on business and financial targets and critical infrastructures.[15]

This may lead to increased governmental intervention in IT developments—particularly in North America, the region of the world most affected by the events of September 11—to ensure that greater weight is given to security considerations in the design, implementation, and operation of IT systems and networks.[16]

NORTH AMERICA WILL, IN GENERAL, DEAL WELL WITH THE STRESSES GENERATED BY THE INFORMATION REVOLUTION

Changes brought on by the information revolution have generated stresses in North American society and will continue to do so. These stresses include

- increasing economic and social disparities brought about by the "digital divide" between the information-rich and the information-poor

- employment disruptions associated with "creative destruction," as new IT-enabled products and services drive out older, less-attractive ones and, often, cause the economic eclipse of the companies that were producing the old products and services[17]

- challenges to individual privacy, as more and more personal information is transferred into databases accessible over the Internet or available to government agencies, and as sensors surveilling human activity become increasingly prevalent.

In general, North American society has dealt well with these stresses; it will continue to do so, by virtue of

- a culture that readily accepts change and, generally speaking, views it as an opportunity rather than a threat[18]

- a labor market that, most of the time, has created new jobs faster than old jobs have disappeared, combined with a work force that accepts frequent changes in employment

- a culture that, for better or worse, accepts wide disparities in income, emphasizing equality of opportunity rather than equality of outcome[19,20]

- a population that, at least up until now, has been willing to accept some loss in privacy in return for personalized products and services.[21]

NOTES

[1]Throughout this report, by "North America" we mean the United States and Canada. We discuss Mexico as part of "Latin America."

[2]Friedman (1999, particularly pp. 298–303) elaborates on these advantageous (for the information revolution) characteristics of North America society.

[3]Canada—with the possible exception of Quebec—is becoming increasingly indistinguishable from the United States in most aspects of life, including its response to the information revolution. Hurtig (2002) documents this increasing Americanization of Canadian life (of which he disapproves) and discusses the forces driving this process. Beatty (2002) reviews the increasing integration of the Canadian and American economies since the Progressive Conservative government of Brian Mulroney came to power in Canada in 1984 and reviews the forces driving further integration.

[4]Along with these strengths, North American has weaknesses as well: for example, its huge legacy communications infrastructure that somewhat slows its adoption of new technology, its tendency sometimes to go it alone regarding standards (e.g., for mobile telephony), etc. These weaknesses will offer opportunities to other IT players outside North America. (The authors thank William Overholt, RAND, for this observation.)

[5]As one measure of this leading position, UNDP (2001, pp. 45–63) creates a "technology achievement index" measuring a country's achievements in the "network age." The United States and Canada both fall into the top group of "leaders," with the United States placing second overall—Finland is first—and Canada eighth, out of 72 countries from all over the world that are quantitatively ranked.

[6]We outline some of the information technology developments that are possible over the next 10 to 20 years in Chapter Two of this report. North America should play a leading role in all of these.

[7]Chapter Two discusses the pivotal role played by "killer applications" in shaping the course of IT developments.

[8]We discuss the general nature of these new business models in Chapter Three of this report.

[9]While North America will continue in the vanguard of the information revolution, not all existing North American companies that are IT leaders today will continue in their leading position throughout the next 10 to 20 years; creative destruction will operate in the future just as it has in the past, so that some of today's leading IT companies will be overcome by new developments and new competitors.

[10]We discuss creative destruction, electronic commerce, information work and information workers, and IT business clusters in Chapter Three of this report.

[11]*BusinessWeek* (2001) provides an overview of the dot-com crash; *The Economist* (2002b) looks at the business and financial crisis in the global telecommunications industry in recent years.

[12]The monthly "Cash Flow" column in the magazine *Red Herring* tracks the rate of investment, by venture capitalists and others, in new IT-related businesses, both in

the United States and globally. The data presented in this column over time clearly show the marked drawdown in such investments since the venture capital investment peak in 2000.

[13]The railroad boom and bust in the 1870s is a classic example of this phenomenon. In the early 1870s, railroads drove economic expansion in the United States and created wealth much as telecom and Internet investment did in the 1990s. In 1873, railroad stocks collapsed, sinking by a third between the end of 1873 and the middle of 1877. But then things turned around, with railroads again powering an expansion. This resumption of growth in railroad-related industries proved to be stable and enduring, paving the way for several decades of U.S. economic growth. (See endnote 26 in Chapter Three for a longer discussion of the 1870s railroad bubble, its collapse, and the subsequent resumption of long-term technology-driven growth.)

[14]*BusinessWeek* (2001) provides a vision of how IT-related industries will recover from their current malaise and continue to transform the business and financial world—in its words, "unevenly and in stages."

[15]The U.S. government has for some time been concerned regarding the cyberspace-related vulnerabilities of critical U.S. infrastructures. (See, for example, PCCIP, 1997). However, because most of these infrastructures are owned and operated by the private sector and therefore outside of direct government control, the government has thus far been unable to affect much of an improvement in their cyber security. (PCIPB, 2002, gives an assessment of the state of critical infrastructure cyber security today.)

[16]In response to market forces, up until now functionality has almost always been given much greater weight than security in the design of new IT systems and networks and their subsequent implementation and operation. This has led to a situation where security vulnerabilities are commonplace, security incidents are a frequent occurrence, and the business community—except for the financial services industry—has treated these incidents as a "cost of doing business." (See PCIPB, 2002, for an overview of the state of cyberspace security today.)

[17]Not all new IT-enabled products and services survive and prosper in the marketplace—witness the collapse of many dot-com companies in recent years. This adds to the employment disruptions.

[18]Levine (2001) describes the American approach to economic change as emphasizing ambition over security, saying, "For many Americans—particularly the most competent—the hope of getting rich is a more compelling incentive than the fear of becoming poor."

[19]This is somewhat less true today in Canada than in the United States, but, as mentioned earlier, as time goes on, Canada is becoming more and more like the United States.

[20]This is in contrast to Europe, which we discuss in Chapter Eight of this report.

[21]This issue is discussed in Hundley et al. (2001).

THE INFORMATION REVOLUTION IS FOLLOWING A SOMEWHAT DIFFERENT AND MORE DELIBERATE COURSE IN EUROPE

Because of differences in the underlying social, political, and economic climate, the information revolution is following a somewhat different and more deliberate course in Europe than in America, even though the underlying technology is largely the same.[1]

EUROPEANS PLACE MORE EMPHASIS ON WIRELESS

In the technology arena, the European view of the information revolution is similar but not identical to the American view. The Europeans place much more emphasis on wireless technology as enabling mobile gateways to the Internet and as an area where they feel they are currently in the lead.

This European enthusiasm for wireless has been tempered somewhat by Europeans recent experience with "third-generation" (3G) wireless.[2] Many Europeans have been counting on their current lead in 3G technology to give Europe an edge in the next set of information society developments.[3] Whether this will turn out to be true remains to be seen, in view of the market uncertainties and financial difficulties currently facing the leading European wireless and telecommunications companies engaged in 3G development. Simply put, the initial market projections for 3G telephony appear to have been considerably overblown, and the European telecommunications companies appear to have paid excessive amounts for their 3G licenses.[4] This could well thwart Europe's 3G ambitions.[5]

THE INFORMATION REVOLUTION IN EUROPE IS DEVELOPING IN A DIFFERENT CLIMATE

While the technology underpinnings are largely the same, the social, political, and economic climate in which the information revolution is developing in Europe differs in important ways from that in America.[6]

Differing European and American Approaches to Economic and Social Change

Economic and social change seems to come easier in America than in Europe, sometimes much easier.[7] As individuals, Europeans are on average much more risk averse than are Americans when it comes to economic change.[8] As a society, Europe is generally distrustful of major economic or social changes. As a result, many more obstacles to change have arisen in Europe than in America, including a financial sector that is less supportive of small startup companies.

The Greater Importance Europeans Attach to Economic and Social Equity

Another key difference between Europe and America emphasized in the conference discussions is the much greater importance Europeans attach to economic and social equity. Europeans place a much greater value on equality of outcomes than do Americans, who value equality of opportunity rather than of outcomes and are more accepting of "winner takes all" situations. This greater European concern for economic and social equity may be inconsistent with the large rewards often associated with successful risk-taking in dynamic business sectors.

The European Desire for "Convergence"

Closely related to the European desire for economic and social equity is a desire for "convergence" among the countries of Europe, where by convergence is meant the reduction of differences in economic prosperity among the various European nations—including those not yet admitted to the European Union. This is another area in which America clearly differs from Europe. Most American states don't want to "converge" with other states; they want to get ahead of those states.

Some observers, Europeans as well as Americans, wonder if the pursuit of economic convergence is consistent with full exploitation of the opportunities afforded by the new information technologies.[9]

Differing Trade-Offs Between Market Forces and Government Policies

Europe and America take differing approaches to balancing these factors: the United States gives market forces more of a free rein; Europe leans harder on government policy to produce socially desirable ends. This is clearly related to the U.S. emphasis on economic efficiency versus the European emphasis on economic and social equity.

A Greater European Emphasis on Top-Down Planning

Closely related to this is a greater European emphasis on top-down planning by governmental and business elites (often working in close conjunction), both on a national basis and by the European Union. The United States relies much more on bottom-up, market-driven, private-sector planning, with the government role limited to preparing the playing field and providing ground rules for competition and innovation, but not trying to second-guess where the breakthroughs and developments will occur.

The European Emphasis on Sustainability

A recurring theme in Europe today is the question of sustainability: whether the information revolution will hinder or enhance sustainable—in environmental and economic terms—development.[10] Most Europeans attach considerable importance to achieving sustainable development.[11] Many also acknowledge, however, that such a future is unlikely to come about without significant intervention by governments and other agents of stability and social change.

THE COURSE OF THE INFORMATION REVOLUTION IN EUROPE IS SOMEWHAT DIFFERENT

As a result of this different climate, the information revolution is following a somewhat different course in Europe than in America:

- Because substantial change in the patterns of economic activity is required to take full advantage of the new information technologies, with new companies arising and some old companies falling by the wayside, with new jobs appearing on the scene and some old jobs disappearing, the differing European and American attitudes toward such change could be quite consequential. In particular, the process of "creative destruction" by which new technologies and business paradigms replace their predecessors as the information revolution progresses is likely to proceed more slowly in Europe than in the United States.[12]

- The "winner takes all" mentality in the United States has led to a very aggressive pursuit of new IT-related business opportunities, particularly by small startup companies financed initially by venture capital. The European economic and social equity emphasis is leading to a more subdued approach to these same opportunities in much of Europe.[13]

- The top-down planning mentality in Europe, with governments playing a major role, reinforces this slower approach because deliberate, top-down planning almost always takes longer, particularly when governments are involved.[14]

- As a corollary to all of the above, when a new technology opportunity or economic arrangement manifests itself, the American approach is to try it out and see what happens. The European approach is to first assess the likely consequences, to make sure nothing bad—or at least not too bad—will happen, before trying it out.[15]

All of this means that up to now the information revolution has been proceeding more deliberately in Europe than in America, with the United States in the vanguard in most (but not all) IT-related areas and Europe following along somewhat behind. This is likely to continue for at least the next few years, if not longer, Europe's current lead in wireless telephony notwithstanding.[16]

WILL, OR MUST, EUROPE BECOME MORE LIKE AMERICA? MAYBE YES, MAYBE NO

Given all these differences between Europe and America, what does the future hold? Driven by the forces of the information revolution and globalization, will Europe become more like America? To succeed in the information age, must Europe become more like America? There is no consensus on these questions among knowledgeable observers, European or American.[17]

Some observers—notably European—feel that although Europe is and will likely remain attached to the ideals of social equity and inter-European convergence, influences already afoot will inevitably make Europe more like America: more tolerant of disparities in income and wealth within nations and more realistic about the fact that all nations cannot achieve similar rates of economic development. The completion of the European market will increase competition within Europe.[18] The European Union Stability Pact will limit government deficits, and competition for employment and investment will restrain taxation. European Union enlargement will only heighten this competition. Similarly, adoption of a common currency will speed the integration of European financial markets and intensify competition for investment.

In this view, the result of these forces will be to limit the capacity of European governments to pursue social equality. Although European governments will remain officially committed to equality of outcome among their citizens, the reality will be increasingly laissez-faire policies that will accelerate the incentives for and increase the rewards of successful exploitation of information technology. In short, Europe will become more like America.[19]

Other observers strongly reject this view, warning against generalizations that suggest that Europe shares a single approach to preserving social equity. In fact, they say, there are many social-economic models within Europe, and some of them, at least, will prove able to withstand the American challenge.[20] In these observers' view, Europe will be able to maintain its cherished differences.

SOME EUROPEANS VIEW AMERICAN DOMINANCE AS PART OF THE "DARK SIDE" OF THE INFORMATION REVOLUTION

The U.S. dominance of the information revolution is brought up frequently by European observers. Many instances of this dominance are cited, including U.S. control of the development of the Internet, the procedures for assignment of Internet domain names, and Hollywood's dominance of film and television entertainment and its effect on European and other non-U.S. cultures.

Directly related to this U.S. dominance are issues of trust in and dependence on the United States—in European eyes, there is too much need for trust and too much dependence. According to observers, many Europeans are worried about their increasing need to trust information systems built (or integrated) in the United States on which their business and governmental operations and critical infrastructures depend. Europeans wonder if deliberate security "back doors" or flaws are inserted into these U.S.-supplied information systems to facilitate U.S. governmental and commercial intelligence collection.

Because of these trust and dependency issues, many Europeans view the United States as part of the "dark side" of the information revolution.[21] This could have important implications for future U.S.-European relations.

NOTES

[1] The picture of the information revolution in Europe presented here is based largely on material presented during the RAND/NIC conference on the information revolution in Europe, held in Belgium in April 2001. The proceedings of this conference are presented in Hundley et al. (2001).

[2] First-generation (1G) wireless denotes the voice-only analog cellular phones (and supporting networks) that have been around since the 1970s and were deployed widely in North America, Europe, and other areas in the 1980s and early 1990s. Second-generation (2G) wireless denotes the digital cellular phones and networks that were deployed beginning in the mid-1990s and are widespread throughout the world today. As well as voice, 2G wireless can provide limited data services (e.g., text messaging). Third-generation (3G) wireless is the designation applied to multimedia (voice, data, and video) cellular phones and networks that will be deployed over the next few years. These 3G cellular phones have a much larger bandwidth than the 2G phones and are expected to provide functionally useful Internet connectivity to mobile users. Between 2G and 3G wireless is enhanced second-generation (2.5G) wireless; these

cellular phones have a bandwidth between that of 2G and 3G and can provide more-advanced data services than does 2G.

[3]"Information society" is a loosely defined term used to signify a society in which networked information and communication media are having a profound effect on many aspects of life.

[4]Several European telecommunications companies are in considerable financial difficulty today because of the very large sums they paid for their 3G licenses. See, for example, *The Economist* (2001) and Baker and Clifford (2002).

[5]See *The Economist* (2002a) for a discussion of this point, and Connell (2002) for a status report on the difficulties facing Europe's 3G efforts.

[6]This summary description of the social, political, and economic climate in Europe necessarily oversimplifies, for purposes of brevity, the nuanced discussion of the many "climatic" variations occurring across Europe that is contained in Hundley et al. (2001).

[7]This was repeatedly emphasized during RAND's European conference discussions.

[8]In a recent article, Levine (2001) describes the American approach to economic change as emphasizing ambition over security, saying, "For many Americans—particularly the most competent—the hope of getting rich is a more compelling incentive than the fear of becoming poor."

[9]This point was made by some participants, European as well as American, in RAND's April 2001 conference.

[10]This was a recurring theme among the European participants in RAND's April 2001 conference. No consensus was reached on this question.

[11]Sustainable development is much less of a concern today in the United States. Hilsenrath (2002) summarizes current U.S. views, pro and con, on this subject.

[12]This was noted several times during RAND's April 2001 conference.

[13]In much, but not all, of Europe. During the 1990s, for example, there was an explosion of startup IT companies in Sweden and Finland.

[14]Not all top-down, government-directed/influenced planning is bad. Historically, some has proven quite valuable and has actually sped up economic development: e.g., the U.S. interstate highway system, the benefits of the common-format VHS system in conflict with Betamax, the systematic creation of high-tech industrial parks in various nations, and the Asian government-directed/influenced growth rates that have averaged about three times Western growth rates (and except for Japan still do). (We thank RAND colleague William Overholt for this observation.)

[15]This point was made, in exactly these words, by one of the European participants in RAND's April 2001 conference.

[16]As noted earlier, the leading European wireless and telecommunications companies attempting to exploit this lead face major market uncertainties and financial difficul-

ties. This could well thwart Europe's 3G ambitions. See, for example, *The Economist* (2001 and 2002a) and Baker and Clifford (2002).

[17]Participants in RAND's April 2001 conference discussed these questions intensely, with no consensus emerging among either the Europeans or Americans present.

[18]"Completion of the European market" is a phase that is commonly applied (in Europe) to a constellation of public- and private-sector actions that will eventually result in the European Union becoming a single market—for goods, services, labor, and finance. Most official barriers to the flow of goods, services, and labor within the European Union were eliminated in 1992. The fixing of exchange rates in 1998 removed further barriers to intra-European transactions. The arrival of the euro in January 2002 was yet another step in this direction. European governments continue to harmonize national policies to make commerce and finance increasingly border-less. And private companies are gradually realigning and relocating operations to take advantage of the opportunities afforded by the expanded European market. The full implications of economic and financial liberalization that has swept Europe in recent years have not yet been felt, and it is in this sense that the single European market is not yet "complete."

[19]As an extension of this view, some participants in the April 2001 conference pointed out that the generation that will do the most to shape the course of the information revolution in Europe—today's young people—was not represented at that conference. Conference participants, they asserted, know little about the attitudes of young people toward information technology, work, or society. They speculated that members of the younger generation of Europeans will become (or already are) more like their American contemporaries than their elders are or will be.

[20]As an extension of this view, many European participants in the April 2001 conference believed that although IT will increase homogeneity within Europe and between it and other developed nations in some respects, it will enhance heterogeneity in others (e.g., harmonized laws but mass customization).

[21]This "dark side" aspect of U.S. dominance of the information revolution was brought up frequently by European participants in RAND's April 2001 conference. This surprised many if not most of the U.S. attendees at the conference.

MANY ASIA-PACIFIC NATIONS ARE POISED TO DO WELL IN THE INFORMATION REVOLUTION, SOME ARE NOT

ASIA-PACIFIC NATIONS VARY GREATLY IN THEIR INFORMATION REVOLUTION POSTURES

How goes the information revolution in the Asia-Pacific region?[1] That question is best answered in two parts: To what extent do Asian countries *use* information technology, and to what extent do they *produce* IT hardware and software? Not surprisingly, they vary greatly on both counts, and not all the big users are big producers and vice versa. Figure 9.1 illustrates the latter point—showing (1) the major IT user and producer nations, (2) China and to a lesser extent India (rapidly emerging as important IT users and producers), and (3) other nations that are lagging behind—and provides a reference for the following discussion.[2]

Several Asia-Pacific Nations Are Doing Well Today in the Information Revolution

Among the Asia-Pacific nations, Japan, South Korea, Singapore, and Taiwan are today both big users and big producers of IT. Australia, Hong Kong, and New Zealand are big users but not big producers, whereas Malaysia, the Philippines, and Thailand are big producers but not big users.[3] All these nations can be said to be doing relatively well today insofar as the information revolution is concerned.

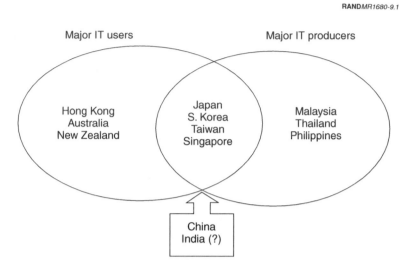

RAND*MR1680-9.1*

Figure 9.1—IT Users and Producers in the Asia-Pacific Region

Regarding IT usage, in 2000 Internet penetration in South Korea, Hong Kong, Japan, and Australia (in that order) exceeded even the U.S. level, with Singapore, Taiwan, and New Zealand (in that order) not far behind.[4,5] In contrast to the situation in the United States, however, most Internet usage in Asia today is by businesses, not from the home.[6] Usage by businesses, though, is not terribly sophisticated. Functions like email, supply chain management, and office automation dominate.[7]

Today the Asia-Pacific Region Is a Much More Significant Global IT Producer Than a Consumer

Japan, Singapore, Taiwan, South Korea, Malaysia, Thailand, and the Philippines are all major IT producers, with IT exports being a major fraction of the total economy in all these nations except Japan.[8] Indeed, the Asia-Pacific region is a much more significant global IT producer than a consumer. It accounts for more than 80 percent of the total world output of the following IT products: desktop PCs, notebook PCs, cathode-ray tube (CRT) monitors, flat-panel displays, modems, network interface cards, hard disk drives, mouses, key-boards, televisions, game boxes, mobile phones, PDAs, entry-level servers, hubs, and switches.[9]

Asia is equally dominant in its output share of critical components and materials used in the IT industry. For the world's semiconductor industry, Asia produces more than 70 percent of all bare silicon material, more than 90 percent of epoxy resin for integrated circuitry (IC) packaging, more than 80 percent of memory semiconductors (DRAMs, SRAMs, and flash memory), and more than 75 percent of outsourced manufactured semiconductors. Other critical IT parts made primarily in Asia include a wide range of passive components (resistors, diodes, capacitors), connectors, sockets, switched power supplies, liquid crystal display (LCD) panels, printed circuit boards, and casings.[10] Asia's share of global IT hardware output is not only large but is still on a steep upward climb, as a growing number of ever-higher value parts and products get outsourced to the region for production.[11]

Asian Nations Generally Follow the "Japan Model" in the Evolution of Their IT Production Activities

Asian IT producers have generally followed the "Japan model" of progressively sophisticated production technology, beginning with labor-intensive, low-value manufacturing. The model, shown in Figure 9.2, can be seen as a compromise between European top-down regulation and U.S. bottom-up entrepreneurialism.[12]

Because they all follow the Japan model, the industrial sophistication of the various Asian IT-producing countries can be compared according to their level in that model, as shown in Table 9.1. South Korean and Taiwanese companies are thus among the more techno-logically advanced and diversified, after Japan, but they face chal-lenges on their road to becoming global IT innovators. At the other end of the spectrum, most Southeast Asian IT producers appear to be stagnating at lower rungs on the production ladder. The reasons include their lack of indigenous IT companies and the rise of China (which we discuss below).[13]

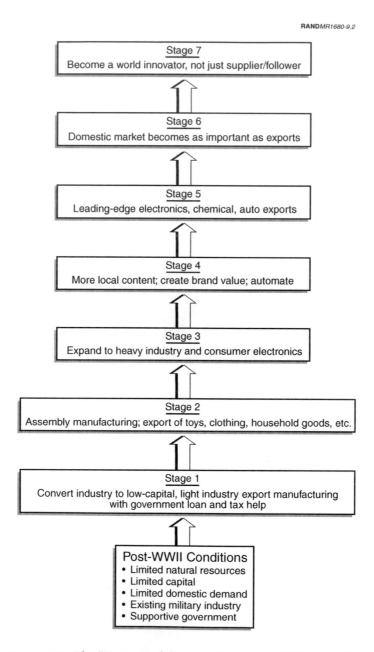

RAND*MR1680-9.2*

Figure 9.2—The "Japan Model" of the Evolution of IT Production

Table 9.1

Sophistication of IT Producers in the Asia-Pacific Region

IT Producer	Stage	IT Ownership	Expertise
Japan	7	Domestic	Consumer electronics, advanced materials and components, IC design and manufacturing, computers
South Korea	6	Domestic	Consumer electronics, phones, peripherals, IC design and manufacturing
Taiwan	5	Domestic	PCs, peripherals, components, IC design and manufacturing, some communications equipment
Singapore	4	Domestic and foreign	Disk drives, PC peripheral assembly, some IC manufacturing
Malaysia	3	Foreign	Disk drives, PC peripheral assembly, cell phone assembly
Thailand	2	Foreign	Disk drives, disk drive component assembly
Philippines	2	Foreign	Peripherals assembly, some software and services

Japan Has Something of a "Split Personality" Today Regarding the Information Revolution

There is no question that Japan is one of the world's leaders in IT today.[14] However, much has been written in recent years regarding the rigidities of the Japanese society, economy, and government, the difficulties this causes Japan in coping with rapid, profound change, such as that brought on by globalization and the information revolution, and the resulting stagnation of the Japanese economy since the early 1990s.[15] This societal rigidity does not bode well for Japan's ability to respond effectively to future challenges posed by the information revolution.

On the other hand, some observers have noted a recent emergence of individualism and entrepreneurship in some sectors of the Japanese IT industry.[16] If this nascent trend persists and spreads, it could ensure the future vitality of that industry, in spite of the rigidities in the larger society.

China and India Are of Special Note as Rapidly Emerging IT Users and Producers

Clearly defined clusters of IT industry are already developing in China and India, although IT output is far from being a major component of either country's economy.[17,18] Both nations are following the early stages of the Japan model in the evolution of their IT production activities, starting low on the value-added chain. Both governments, especially China, have policies in place to encourage foreign companies to invest and produce locally, as well as incentives and allowances to foster homegrown IT companies. An assortment of lower-end hardware manufacturing dominates today in China, while back-office services and software outsourcing dominate in India.[19]

China will almost surely advance to later stages in IT industry development, in the process possibly leapfrogging many nations that today are more advanced but burdened by the inertia created by legacy infrastructures. The major driving forces in China are the size and potential of its local market and the almost endless availability of cheap labor, both of which attract foreign investment.[20] In recent years, China has become the IT manufacturing base of choice, with a number of Taiwanese and Hong Kong IT companies beginning to transfer their manufacturing operations there—a trend that is likely not only to continue but also to accelerate—and has rapidly attracted a large, increasingly advanced IT knowledge base, some of it from expatriate Chinese returning home after receiving technical training overseas.[21,22]

India shares some of China's potential; its software production has increased fiftyfold over the past 10 years.[23] However, experts assess the environment as not being sufficiently "ripe" yet for breakout IT development in India, pointing out that software created there has negligible copyright protection today, services are hard to scale, the domestic market is tiny, and IT manufacturing has not taken root. These experts see political instability and a discouraging venture formation environment as added hurdles.[24] As a result, India faces substantial talent outflow problems.[25]

Other Asian Nations Are Lagging Well Behind

Many other Asian nations are lagging well behind (e.g., Bhutan, Cambodia, Indonesia, Laos, Mongolia, Myanmar, Nepal, Pakistan, Sri Lanka, Vietnam, and the nations of Central Asia).[26] These nations have low levels of Internet penetration and usage, and little or no IT production activity. Not only are they lagging behind today; little is occurring to improve their future situations insofar as the information revolution is concerned.

THE IMPACT OF THE INFORMATION REVOLUTION ON POLITICS AND GOVERNANCE IN THE ASIA-PACIFIC REGION VARIES WIDELY FROM NATION TO NATION

The information revolution is affecting politics and governance in the Asia-Pacific region largely through two mechanisms:

- Bottom-up actions and initiatives of citizens, civil society, non-governmental organizations, and political parties, facilitated and enabled by IT, ranging from organizing minor protests of government policies all the way to overthrowing sitting regimes.[27]

- Top-down initiatives of governments that use IT to deliver information and services, generally termed "electronic government," or "e-government."

Governments are having a major impact in both of these areas: in the latter as the initiator and driving force; in the former by their acceptance of or opposition to these bottom-up initiatives.[28]

Information Technology Has Had an Impact on Politics in Some Asian Nations Thus Far, but Not in Others

Asian nations are often classed as one-party states or liberal democracies insofar as their approach to politics is concerned.[29] All of the liberal democracies in Asia have virtually no restrictions on Internet access and online political use and content, whereas the one-party states have a range of restrictions, as summarized in Table 9.2.[30]

Table 9.2

**Degree of Restrictions on Internet Political Use and Content,
by Type of Government**

States Having Restrictions of the Following Type (one-party states in *italics*; liberal democracies in Roman)			
Severe	**Significant**	**Moderate**	**Negligible**
Severe restrictions on online political content and usage through limits on access	Significant restrictions on Internet access or online political content and usage, or both	Promotion of public Internet access; moderate restrictions on political content and use	Promotion of Internet access, and few or no restrictions on online political content and use
Myanmar *North Korea*	*China* *Vietnam*	*Singapore*	Australia India Indonesia Japan *Malaysia* Philippines South Korea Thailand

One might think that IT would have a significant impact on politics in all of those Asian nations with few restrictions on Internet access, use, and content, but little or no impact in nations with significant restrictions. Thus far, this has not been the case. IT has had a significant impact on politics in some one-party states and liberal democracies but not in others, as indicated in Table 9.3.[31] The reasons for this impact, or lack thereof, are largely specific to each country.[32]

IT Is Reshaping the Way Asia-Pacific Governments Conduct the Business of Governance: More in Some Nations Than in Others

Several Asian governments routinely place within the top 10 countries in the world in surveys of e-government activities; these include Australia, Singapore, Hong Kong, New Zealand, and Taiwan.[33] Other countries are devoting significant amounts of time and resources to e-government but have not yet reached a level of global sophistication; those include Thailand, the Philippines, and Malaysia. Coun-

Table 9.3

IT Influence on Politics Versus Government Type

Influence of Information Technology on Politics	Type of Government	
	One-Party States	Liberal Democracies
Visible influence	China Indonesia Malaysia	Philippines South Korea
No significant influence	Myanmar North Korea Singapore	Australia India Japan

tries such as India and China have remarkable pockets of innovation in local government but are in the early stages overall.[34] Other nations, including North Korea, Myanmar, Vietnam, and Indonesia, have not developed robust e-government programs.[35]

WHAT DOES THE FUTURE HOLD FOR THE ASIA-PACIFIC REGION?

Over Time, China Should Emerge as a Major IT Player in Asia and the World

As noted earlier, in recent years China has become the IT manufacturing base of choice, for Asian, North American, and even European companies. The major driving forces behind this trend are the size and potential of the local Chinese market and the almost endless availability of cheap labor, both of which foreign investors find very attractive. As a corollary, China is also beginning to attract a large knowledge base of increasingly advanced know-how, some of it from expatriate Chinese returning home after receiving technical training overseas.

These trends will almost certainly continue, and could even accelerate now that China has joined the World Trade Organization. China should continue advancing to later stages in IT industry development and, over time, become a major IT player not only in Asia but also in the world, in the process possibly leapfrogging many nations that today are more advanced but burdened by the inertia created by legacy infrastructures.

This assumes continued peaceful relations between China and the United States and a continued peaceful, gradual liberalization of China's government. The impact of IT should further this liberalization, through its enabling of bottom-up political activity and top-down e-government initiatives.[36]

Other Asian Nations Currently Leading in IT Will Define Their Futures by Their Responses to China's Growing IT Role

South Korea, Taiwan, and the leading IT nations in Southeast Asia achieved their current positions initially by serving as low-cost manufacturing outposts for North American, European, and Japanese electronics and IT companies, beginning with the manufacture of components and gradually working up the IT value-added chain, beginning under foreign ownership and gradually transitioning (in some but not all of these nations) to domestic ownership. This process took several decades.[37]

The emergence of China as the new low-cost, mass-market manufacturing outpost of choice in Asia changes the IT playing field on which these other Asian nations must now operate. Already, many Taiwanese and Hong Kong IT companies have begun to transfer their manufacturing operations to China, at the component, subsystem, and even system level; Japanese companies are beginning to follow suit.[38] And nations such as Singapore, Malaysia, Thailand, and the Philippines have begun to lose contract manufacturing business to companies in China with lower-cost plants.[39]

This is not necessarily a zero-sum game, however; China's IT gains do not have to be losses for other Asian nations.[40] For these other nations to survive as viable players in the IT world, they must redefine their business models, carving out value-added niches that can withstand the Chinese onslaught. Some of them, such as South Korea and Taiwan, may succeed by retaining design and high-level engineering capabilities at home while outsourcing manufacturing operations to China.[41] Other Asian nations, however, that have not yet advanced to the design and high-level engineering level in their IT operations may have substantial difficulty.

Japan's Future Course Is Unclear: It Could Continue as a Leader in IT or Gradually Fall Behind

We mentioned earlier the societal rigidities that Japan has displayed in recent years and the resulting stagnation of the Japanese economy throughout the 1990s. If this condition persists, it could lead Japan gradually to fall behind the nations in the vanguard of the information revolution.

On the other hand, if the recent emergence of individualism and entrepreneurship in some sectors of the Japanese IT industry, also mentioned earlier, persists and spreads, it would offer hope for the near- to mid-term recovery and long-term vitality of the Japanese IT industry and the larger economy. In this case, Japan would continue as a world leader in IT, albeit with an ever-increasing fraction of its manufacturing operations "offshored" to Japanese-owned facilities in China.

It remains to be seen which of these forces—rigidities in the overall society or nascent individualism and entrepreneurship in the Japanese IT industry—proves stronger.

India's Software and Back-Office Service Industries Should Prosper; However, a Broader Role in the Information Revolution May Be Beyond India's Reach

India has three important advantages in the global IT competition: a plentiful supply of talented IT-trained people; copious numbers of educated, low-cost workers proficient in English; and close ties to the many Indian entrepreneurs in Silicon Valley.[42] These factors should ensure the continued prosperity and growth of the Indian software and back-office service industries, at least over the near- to mid-term.[43] However, going beyond software into IT hardware activities may be difficult, particularly in view of China's growing role in this area.[44] Also, the entire Indian high-tech industry is a small veneer on top of the Indian economy.[45] Much of the nation is still in the agricultural age, not yet having reached the industrial age, let alone the information age. These factors may place any broader role in the information revolution beyond India's reach.

Most of Today's Laggards Will Continue to Lag

Most of these lagging nations (e.g., Bhutan, Cambodia, Indonesia, Laos, Mongolia, Myanmar, Nepal, Pakistan, Sri Lanka, Vietnam, and the nations of Central Asia) lack one or more essential elements required to do well in the information revolution.[46] Accordingly, they will continue to lag behind.

NOTES

[1] By the "Asia-Pacific region" we mean Asia, in its entirety, plus Oceania (i.e., Australia, New Zealand, and most of the smaller islands of the Pacific Ocean). Throughout this chapter, we will sometimes use "Asia" or "Asian" as a short form to refer to the entire Asia-Pacific region.

[2] We take this figure from Hachigian and Wu (2003). This entire chapter draws heavily on the data, analysis, and findings presented in that report.

[3] In making these statements, we take as a basic measure of IT use the number of Internet users per 1,000 people. For IT production, we use the value of a nation's IT exports in absolute terms (i.e., in U.S. dollars) and also relative to the size of the nation's economy (i.e., IT exports as a fraction of a nation's total exports and a fraction of its GDP). (See Hachigian and Wu, 2003, for a compilation of such data for nations across the Asia-Pacific region and a detailed discussion of their significance.)

[4] Hachigian and Wu (2003) present the following figures on Internet usage per 1,000 people in Asia in 2000 (compared with that in the United States):

Advanced Nations	Users/ 1K	Emerging Nations	Users/ 1K	Lagging Nations	Users/ 1K
S. Korea	402.7	Brunei	88.8	Kazakhstan	6.7
Hong Kong	382.5	Thailand	37.9	Sri Lanka	6.3
Japan	371.1	Micronesia	33.9	India	4.9
Australia	344.1	Philippines	26.5	Uzbekistan	4.8
U.S.	338.7	PNG[a]	26.3	Solomon Is.	4.5
Singapore	298.7	China	17.8	Vietnam	2.5
Taiwan	255.0	Mongolia	12.5	Nepal	2.2
New Zealand	216.7	Kyrgyzstan	10.5	Bhutan	1.9
Malaysia	159.0	Marshall Is.	9.6	Turkmenistan	1.2
New Caledonia	112.8	Indonesia	9.5	Laos	1.1

NOTE: Asian countries with one Internet user or less per 1,000 people in 2000 are Pakistan, Bangladesh, Cambodia, Tajikistan, and Myanmar.
[a] PNG = Papua New Guinea.

[5] Also relevant, as a rough measure of the overall size of a nation's IT market, is the absolute number of Internet users in a nation. Hachigian and Wu (2003) provide the following figures for this quantity in 2000:

Large	Millions of Users	Medium	Millions of Users	Small	Thou-sands of Users
U.S.	95.4	Indonesia	2.0	Kazakhstan	100.0
Japan	47.1	Philippines	2.0	Kyrgyzstan	51.6
China	22.5	Singapore	1.2	Nepal	50.0
S. Korea	19.0	New Zealand	0.8	Mongolia	30.0
Australia	6.6	Vietnam	0.2	Brunei	30.0
Taiwan	5.7	PNG[a]	0.1	New Caledonia	24.0
India	6.0	Pakistan	0.1	Myanmar	7.0
Malaysia	3.7	Sri Lanka	0.1	Laos	6.0
Hong Kong	2.6	Bangladesh	0.1	Cambodia	6.0
Thailand	2.3	Uzbekistan	0.1	Turkmenistan	6.0

NOTE: Countries with 4,000 users or less are Micronesia, Tajikistan, Solomon Is., and Marshall Is.
[a]PNG = Papua New Guinea.

[6]Only in Japan and South Korea does home usage top business usage today. Hachigian and Wu (2003) discuss the factors limiting home usage in Asia.

[7]See Hachigian and Wu (2003) for further discussion of Internet usage in the Asia-Pacific region, including the factors limiting the sophistication of current business usage.

[8]Hachigian and Wu (2003) provide the following data on high-technology exports from Asia-Pacific nations in 2000:

Country	High-Tech Exports in US$M	High-Tech as a % of Total Exports	High-Tech Exports as a % of GDP
United States	367,919	34.0	3.7
Japan	135,564	28.0	2.8
Singapore	104,614	63.0	113.4
Taiwan	80,837	52.8	26.8
S. Korea	72,012	35.0	15.8
Malaysia	57,494	51.3	64.1
Hong Kong	56,111	23.0	34.5
China	53,349	19.0	4.9
Thailand	49,684	60.7	40.7
Philippines	24,692	59.0	33.0
Australia	22,965	15.0	5.9
Indonesia	9,563	16.0	6.2
New Zealand	1,597	10.0	3.2
India	1,408	2.2	0.3

To avoid misinterpreting these data, Hachigian and Wu (2003) note the following two points:

> (1) A large proportion of Hong Kong's IT exports actually involves production in China by Taiwan-owned companies. Taiwanese companies typically hold their Chinese manufacturing subsidiaries under Hong Kong–based overseas entities to circumvent Taiwanese government restrictions on direct investment in China or ownership of China-based entities. (2) In Singapore's and Malaysia's data, exports are reported in total value, including the value of parts that were imported to, but not produced in, Singapore or Malaysia. For example, a $75 hard-disk drive is exported, but local value-added may have been only $35, because $40 in unassembled components was imported. That explains the unusually high IT export value as a percent of GDP [in Singapore's case, over 100 percent].

[9]See Hachigian and Wu (2003).

[10]See Hachigian and Wu (2003).

[11]According to Hachigian and Wu (2003):

> Applied Materials, the leading world maker of semiconductor manufacturing equipment, notes that in the first quarter of 2002, 71% of its equipment was sold to Asia, compared to 41% in 1996. This is a leading indicator that Asia's semiconductor output will as much as double in the years to come.

[12]This "Japan model" of the evolution of IT production was developed by Hachigian and Wu (2003), from which we take Figure 9.2 and much of the accompanying discussion.

[13]See Hachigian and Wu (2003) for further discussion of these issues.

[14]For example, Hachigian and Wu (2003) list the following Japanese companies that today lead in world market share or product excellence in the areas indicated:

Company	Areas of Excellence
Alps	Magnetic disk drive heads
Canon	Cameras, IC manufacturing equipment, office equipment, optic components
Fujitsu	Servers, mainframes, enterprise systems, office equipment, hardware, and ICs
Hitachi	Enterprise storage, enterprise software, advanced ICs
Kyocera	Advanced chemicals and materials, electronic components
Matsushita	Stereos, TVs, VCRs, DVD players, office equipment
NEC	Advanced ICs, PCs, servers, LCD panels, office equipment
Nintendo	Game boxes
NTT Docomo	Mobile services
Shinkawa	IC manufacturing equipment
Sony	Walkman, cameras, game boxes, notebook PCs, stereos, TVs

Table—continued

Company	Areas of Excellence
Sumitomo	Advanced chemicals and materials for aerospace and electronics, power plants
Tokyo Electron	IC manufacturing equipment
Toppan Printing	Printed circuit boards, IC substrate materials
Toshiba	Notebook PCs, advanced ICs, LCD panels, consumer electronics

[15]Grimond (2002) takes a detailed look at "what ails" the Japanese economy, government, and society today. Iritani (2000) provides a briefer version. Miyashita (1999) specifically discusses how cultural obstacles to individualism, risk-taking, and entrepreneurship in Japan impede the nation's ability to meet the challenges posed by the information revolution.

[16]Lily Wu (private communication, 2002) reports a noticeable emergence of entrepreneurship in the Japanese IT industry since 2000. Also see Ono and Spindle (2000), who describe a recent stirring of individualism in Japan, depicting it as a response to the nation's long slump during the 1990s, and Grimond (2002), who mentions stirrings of individualism among the youth in Japan.

[17]In 2000, IT business clusters satisfying criteria established by Hillner (and adopted by the United Nations Development Programme) existed at Hong Kong (now a Special Administrative Area) in China and at Bangalore in India. (See Hillner, 2000, and UNDP, 2001.) Additional IT clusters have begun emerging in both of these nations since then. *BusinessWeek* (2002b) discusses IT clusters emerging in China, including, in particular, the Zhangiang district of Shanghai. Arunachalam (1999) identifies emerging Indian IT clusters at Mumbai (Bombay) and New Delhi; Bradsher (2002b) describes the IT cluster emerging at Hyderabad.

[18]As shown in note 8 above, in 2000, high-tech exports were 4.9 percent of China's GDP and 0.3 percent of India's. (These numbers have increased significantly since then in both nations.)

[19]See Filkins (2000) for a discussion of India's back-office service industry, in which India is one of the world's leaders.

[20]See Hachigian and Wu (2003) for further discussion of China's IT potential.

[21]According to Hachigian and Wu (2003), semiconductor manufacturers believe China will be the next great center of IT production and consumption. *BusinessWeek* (2002b) gives examples of Taiwan and Hong Kong IT companies that are transferring their manufacturing operations to mainland China. Goodman (2002) explores the broader implications of this trend.

[22]Tempest (2002) describes the Chinese government's recent efforts to lure back Chinese IT expatriates from Silicon Valley; Kaufman (2003) recounts the return of one such expatriate.

[23]According to Hachigian and Wu (2003), India's software exports have risen from $150 million per year 10 years ago to $7.6 billion in the 12 months ending March 2002 (two-thirds of which were bound for the United States).

[24]See Hachigian and Wu (2003).

[25]Noteworthy Indian entrepreneurs are numerous in the United States and responsible for many well-known corporate successes. In 2001, 60 percent of all H-1 visa holders in Silicon Valley were software engineers, with India citizens making up 43 percent of the total. (See Hachigian and Wu, 2003.)

[26]UNDP (2001) presents IT-related data on these and other nations throughout the world, including the Asia-Pacific region.

[27]The most dramatic example of IT's political impact on an Asian nation is Indonesia, where it contributed to the downfall of President Suharto. Hachigian and Wu (2003) discuss this further.

[28]We follow Hachigian and Wu (2003) in using this two-mechanism approach to discuss the effect of IT on politics and governance in the Asia-Pacific region.

[29]We take our definition of these two categories from Hachigian and Wu (2003), who distinguish between

> liberal democracies (that is, those democracies that guarantee individual rights for citizens, particularly freedom of expression and assembly) on the one hand and "one-party" states on the other. The latter category includes a range of countries from "electoral" or illiberal democracies, such as Singapore, to true dictatorships, such as North Korea.

[30]We take this table from Hachigian and Wu (2003), which contains a detailed discussion of the type and degree of restrictions on Internet access, use, and content in each of these nations.

[31]We take this table from Hachigian and Wu (2003).

[32]See Hachigian and Wu (2003) for a detailed discussion of the impact, or lack thereof, of IT on politics in each of these nations, and the reasons why.

[33]Australia and Singapore consistently rank among the most advanced e-government leaders in the world. (See Hachigian and Wu, 2003.)

[34]In China, the real energy for e-government is at the provincial and local levels, where, according to Hachigian and Wu (2003), some Chinese officials are enthusiastically embracing e-government.

[35]Hachigian and Wu (2003) discuss e-government efforts in all the nations mentioned here at length.

[36]Miles (2002) provides a much less sanguine view of China's near-term prospects for continued political liberalization and economic development, emphasizing the many obstacles China must overcome on the way. *Red Herring* (2002) provides a range of both positive and negative views.

[37]For one top-level view of this process, as it occurred in Singapore over several decades, see Lee (2000).

[38]See *BusinessWeek* (2002b).

[39]See Hachigian and Wu (2003).

[40]Recent studies by the Asian Development Bank (Roland-Holst, 2002) and Deutsche Bank (Bhaskaran, 2003) make this point.

[41]Already, their Chinese manufacturing sites are beginning to increase the market share, profitability, and technology investment of Taiwanese and South Korean companies. (Private communication, William Overholt, RAND.)

[42]According to Arunachalam (1999), about 170,000 engineers graduate every year from Indian universities, more than in the United States. There are about 250,000 software professionals in India today, and the several hundred IT companies they work for are well coupled to the Internet.

[43]Rai (2002) describes the current state and near-term prospects of India's software and back-office service industries.

[44]Bradsher (2002a) compares the near-term growth potentials of China and India, and finds India lagging.

[45]According to Arunachalam (1999), less than 1 percent of Indian society is in the information age/high-tech veneer today.

[46]We discuss these essential elements in Chapter Six of this report.

LATIN AMERICA FACES MANY OBSTACLES IN RESPONDING TO THE INFORMATION REVOLUTION: SOME NATIONS WILL RISE TO THE CHALLENGE, OTHERS WILL NOT

TODAY MOST LATIN AMERICAN NATIONS ARE "ALSO-RANS" IN THE INFORMATION REVOLUTION, AS THEY ARE IN THE GLOBAL ECONOMY

Latin America's prospects in the information revolution are closely linked to its performance in the emerging global economy. Its major difficulties are the same in both cases:[1]

- The intrusive role of many Latin American governments in their economies and the often dominating roles of large incumbent, and sometimes protected, local firms

- The sometimes volatile nature of Latin America's financial connections to the richer countries of the world, especially the United States[2]

- The need to train and retain skilled people in Latin America.

In recent years, even decades, Latin America has had problems in all these areas. As a result:

- Latin America is something of an "also-ran" in the global economy, with an average GDP per capita only 31 percent of the Organisation for Economic Cooperation and Development (OECD) average in 1999 and a GDP per capita annual growth rate roughly one-third of the OECD average over the 1975–1999 period.[3] In the increasingly important area of high-tech exports,

Latin America lags well behind North America, Europe, and Asia.[4]

- The Internet and other aspects of the information revolution have come late to Latin America. In 2000, Latin America had roughly 15 million Internet users, compared with 160 million in North America, 105 million in Europe, and 90 million in the Asia-Pacific region; only Africa (3.1 million) and the Middle East (2.4 million) had fewer users.[5] Latin America had only 30 Internet users per 1,000 people that year, compared with more than 700 users per 1,000 people in North America and more than 500 users per 1,000 in Europe.[6] The situation is similar for Internet hosts, where Latin America had 5.6 per 1,000 people in 2000, compared with more than 170 per 1,000 in North America; telephone land-lines, where Latin America had 130 per 1,000 people in 2000 compared with more than 650 per 1,000 in North America; and cell phones, where Latin America had 80 per 1,000 people in 2000 compared with nearly 300 per 1,000 in North America.[7,8] Finally, Latin America's intercontinental Internet links totaled less than 3 Gbps in 2000, compared with more than 83 Gbps for North America, about 60 Gbps for Europe, and about 20 Gbps for Asia.[9]

- E-commerce is in its early stages in Latin America. In 2001, only an estimated 2 percent of Latin American business was transacted electronically (compared with 6 percent in North America). Latin America had 4 percent of the global e-commerce market in 2001, compared with 63 percent for North America, 17 percent for Europe, and 15 percent for Asia.[10]

Today, it is clear that Latin America is an also-ran in the information revolution.

LATIN AMERICAN NATIONS CAN BE DIVIDED INTO "LEADERS," "SUCCESSFUL OUTLIERS," AND THE REST

Insofar as the information revolution is concerned, Latin American nations can be divided today into "leaders," "successful outliers," and the rest.

Argentina, Brazil, Chile, Mexico, and Uruguay Have Been Latin America's Leaders in the Information Revolution in Recent Years

In recent years, Argentina, Brazil, Chile, Mexico, and Uruguay have led Latin America in most measures of IT penetration and usage and in IT-related business and financial developments. Argentina has many young entrepreneurs who are computer proficient,[11] opened up all areas of its telecommunications market to an unlimited number of licensees in November 2000, and, prior to its recent financial difficulties, appeared to be developing indigenous venture capital.[12] Brazil leads the rest of Latin America in electronic banking[13] and in e-commerce in general;[14] has led in attracting foreign venture capital; appears to be leading, although still in the early stages, in developing indigenous venture capital; and has developed a number of university-related IT business incubator programs.[15]

Chile has the most competitive telecommunications market in Latin America, followed by Uruguay, Brazil, and Argentina.[16] Chile has taken the lead in protecting IT-related intellectual property rights and has a secondary school *Enlaces* (links) program that will eventually introduce more IT-interested students into the already successful higher education system.[17] Uruguay has a growing indigenous software industry, exploiting its educated workforce.[18]

Mexico is a somewhat special case in Latin America because of its connections to the United States. It has developed two IT-related "clusters"—one at the Monterrey Technical Institute, which has 27 branch campuses and an innovative virtual learning program, and one at "Silicon *Valle*," where IT startups are beginning to thrive.[19]

Mexico also has one important "pull" factor that is unique. The just-in-time inventory needs of the *maquiladoras* on its northern border—processing operations, mostly in consumer electronics, whose inputs can be imported duty free provided all the products are exported—provide a powerful incentive to use IT.[20]

These five nations have in recent years provided IT-related leadership examples to the rest of Latin America. Of these nations, Mexico and Chile continue to do well today, whereas Argentina, Uruguay, and Brazil have recently suffered financial difficulties—in Argentina's case, grave difficulties—that put future economic development in jeopardy.[21]

A Few Latin American Nations Are "Successful Outliers" Regarding the Information Revolution

Several of the mostly small island states in the Caribbean—including the Cayman Islands, the Bahamas, St. Barts, Aruba, the British Virgin Islands, and the U.S. Virgin Islands—are "successful outliers" compared with the rest of Latin America insofar as the information revolution is concerned. They have per capita incomes among the highest in Latin America and are much further along in IT penetration and use. These outliers share several preconditions: their governments are founded on trust and transparency; and they have a well-established rule of law, high literacy rates, economic cultures in which business can prosper, populations fluent in English, and, perhaps most important, political stability.[22]

In Central America, Costa Rica is an IT outlier. Intel has based an assembly plant there, which has had a major impact on Costa Rican employment and growth. In attracting Intel, Costa Rica had advantages similar to the Caribbean islands: a good rule of law; a population that mostly has a "working" knowledge of English;[23] a program to wire every school in the country, so that much of the younger population will soon become computer and Internet savvy; and a sizable number of trained engineers available to work in the Intel plant or in supporting industries. Moreover, Costa Rica has a business school, INCAE, founded with help from the Harvard Business School. Costa Rica has, in effect, created an IT *maquiladora.*[24]

Even though they are doing well themselves in the information revolution, because they are small and removed geographically from the mainstream of Latin America, Costa Rica and these Caribbean nations do not provide leadership examples to the rest of Latin America; they are information revolution outliers, not leaders.

The Rest of the Latin American Nations Are Following Along Behind—Sometimes Way Behind

The rest of the Latin American nations lag behind these leaders and successful outliers, often way behind. These other nations have lower numbers of Internet users and Internet hosts (relative to their populations), sometimes far lower, and limited international Internet bandwidth.[25] The situation is particularly dire for the nations on the Andean ridge (e.g., Bolivia, Ecuador, Peru), those torn by internal guerrilla conflicts (e.g., Colombia), and impoverished island nations of the Caribbean (e.g., Haiti).

LATIN AMERICA FACES MANY OBSTACLES IN EXPLOITING OPPORTUNITIES OFFERED BY THE INFORMATION REVOLUTION

These obstacles include the following:[26]

- A government role in the economy that today appears to be more of an impediment than an advantage in many Latin American nations.[27]

- Privileged positions for large, old-economy firms that often impede the development of markets by new IT-related firms.

- A financial system in many Latin American nations that is not conducive to IT-related startups.[28]

- Difficulties in paying for e-commerce purchases (due to lack of credit cards in many Latin American nations) and delivering purchased goods (due to lack of trusted delivery infrastructures).[29]

- Shortages of skilled people required to produce, operate, and use IT in many Latin American nations, and to perform knowledge work in general, because of deficiencies in the educational systems[30] and "brain drain" losses, primarily to North America.[31]

- As a result of these brain-drain losses, competition from Miami-based companies for the Spanish language–content Internet market.[32]

- A pronounced digital divide, even in the leading Latin American nations, due partially to income disparities and to deficient electric and telecommunications infrastructures in rural areas.[33]

- A propensity for frequent financial crises, associated with instabilities in international capital flows into and out of Latin America.[34,35]

All in all, the business and social climate in Latin America is much less hospitable to the information revolution than in North America or Europe, or in many parts of Asia.

WHAT DOES THE FUTURE HOLD FOR LATIN AMERICA? PROBABLY MORE OF THE SAME

Although the numbers of Internet end users and host computers are growing faster in Latin America than the world averages, the gap between this region and the world's IT leaders is, in the view of experts, not likely to close.[36]

However, in the leading Latin American nations, the Internet appears poised to accelerate economic development but at the price of greater income disparities.[37] Mexico and Chile should continue to do well in the information revolution; so may many of the currently successful outliers (e.g., Costa Rica and some of the Caribbean nations)—assuming that all these nations avoid financial crises.[38]

Argentina has been devastated, not only economically but also socially, by its current financial crisis. It could be many years before it recovers. Until then, progress in the information revolution (or in other areas of economic development) is unlikely.[39]

Brazil and Uruguay are also undergoing financial difficulties today, albeit mild compared with those that in Argentina. How these difficulties are resolved will have much to do with determining how these two nations fare over the next few years insofar as the information revolution is concerned.[40]

The rest of the Latin American nations will most likely continue to follow on behind, as they are doing today—some of them well behind.

In all these nations, the presence or absence of individuals in key public- and private-sector positions who network together to push the information revolution forward—termed "information revolutionaries" by one expert—will be an important shaper of a country's IT future.[41]

NOTES

[1]The chapter draws heavily on the views expressed during RAND's November 2000 conference on the information revolution in Latin America. (See Treverton and Mizell, 2001.)

[2]In the past decade, Latin America's connections to capital from outside the region has been quite problematic because Latin America has been at the mercy of external financial developments, leading to financial crises in Mexico in 1994–1995; in Argentina beginning in the late 1990s, continuing today, and spreading to Uruguay; and, most recently, in Brazil. (See *The Economist*, 2002d, for a recent assessment of this situation.)

[3]In 1999, the OECD nations had an average GDP per capita of $22,000, while the value for Latin America and the Caribbean was $6,880. Over the 1975–1999 period, the GDP per capita annual growth rate was 2.0 percent in the OECD nations and only 0.6 percent in Latin America. (See UNDP, 2001, p. 181.)

[4]In 1998–1999, only three Latin American nations were in the top 30 leading exporters of high-tech products: Mexico (11th, $38 billion), Brazil (27th, $4 billion), and Costa Rica (30th, $3 billion). Mexico was well behind the high-tech export leader that year— the United States, with $206 billion. (See UNDP, 2001, p. 42.)

[5]See Treverton and Mizell (2001), p. 7.

[6]See Treverton and Mizell (2001), p. xiii.

[7]See UNDP (2001), pp. 60–63.

[8]These average numbers mask large variations across Latin America. For example, Bolivia and Ecuador both had 0.3 Internet hosts per 1,000 people in 2000, and Uruguay had 19.6; Paraguay had 55 telephone landlines per 1,000 people in 1999, and Uruguay had 271; and Ecuador had 31 cell phones per 1,000 people in 1999, and Venezuela had 143. (See UNDP, 2001, pp. 60–63.)

[9]See Treverton and Mizell (2001), p. 10.

[10]See Oakes (2002).

[11]Many of these young Argentinean entrepreneurs are of immigrant origin, although not first generation. (See Treverton and Mizell, 2001, p. 45.)

[12]See Treverton and Mizell (2001), pp. 28–29.

[13]See Lipschultz (2001).

[14]See Treverton and Mizell (2001), p. 35.

[15]See Treverton and Mizell (2001), pp. xix, 22, 28, 44.

[16]See Treverton and Mizell (2001), p. 28.

[17]In 1992, Catholic University in Chile began a project to develop and evaluate an elementary school network called *Enlaces*. The project aimed to enhance efficiency, quality, and equity in education and to "integrate the children into the culture." By the end of 2000, 100 percent of Chilean middle and high schools and 50 percent of grammar schools had Internet-connected labs. *Enlaces* is comprehensive in that it covers curriculum development and teacher training and collaboration as well as hardware and software. It was intended from the beginning to cover the entire nation, and, as such, different universities are responsible for different regions of the nation. (See Treverton and Mizell, 2001, pp. 12–13.)

[18]See Treverton and Mizell (2001), p. 29.

[19]See Treverton and Mizell (2001). The 125 firms in Silicon *Valle* are all foreign owned—four-fifths American and the rest Asian.

[20]Foreign direct investment in Mexico, much of it focused on these *maquiladoras*, has grown from $4 billion to $13 billion annually since NAFTA, the North American Free Trade Agreement, came into effect in 1995. (See Treverton and Mizell, 2001, p. xviii.)

[21]We return to these financial difficulties later in this chapter.

[22]It should be noted, however, that these countries' IT advances were driven by the needs of their commerce—tourism and banking (including in some cases, unfortunately, money laundering)—not the other way around. The existing electronic infrastructure associated with these industries made it easier for them to incorporate new information technologies. (See Treverton and Mizell, 2001, p. 30.)

[23]To attract Intel, Costa Rica took the politically risky step of committing to teach English in its primary schools. (See Treverton and Mizell 2001, p. 31.)

[24]See Treverton and Mizell (2001), p. 31.

[25] See UNDP (2001), pp. 60–63, and Treverton and Mizell (2001), pp. 5–14, for quantitative Internet-related data on all the Latin American nations.

[26]These are discussed in more detail in Treverton and Mizell (2001).

[27]See Treverton and Mizell (2001), pp. xix–xx, 33–37, for further discussion of this issue.

[28]Many of the IT-related startups currently conducting business in Latin America were organized and financed outside of the region. Others serve the region from external locations (e.g., Miami). (See Treverton and Mizell, 2001, p. xvii.)

[29]For these reasons, business-to-business e-commerce may have a more promising future than business-to-consumer e-commerce in many Latin America nations today. (See Treverton and Mizell, 2001.)

[30]Education is a primary obstacle to exploiting IT-related opportunities in many Latin American nations. Dropout rates are high, repeat rates in primary school are very high, teaching materials are outdated, and the worst teachers are in the primary schools. At the university level, teachers are ill paid, and so moonlighting and part-time teaching are the norm. Unions and bureaucracy create barriers to innovation, and the upper classes send their children to private schools. (See Treverton and Mizell, 2001, pp. xix, 40–42, 45–47.)

[31]In much of northern South America, in particular, skilled people who can leave do leave, most often for the United States. They are pushed out by violence, by the lack of opportunities, and by populist politics that discourage innovation and individual enrichment. In the process, Miami is becoming a kind of economic and cultural "capital" of Latin America. (See Treverton and Mizell, 2001, p. xix.)

[32]Given the large market for Spanish-language Internet content, not only in Latin America but also throughout the entire Spanish-speaking world—only 2 percent of Web content is now in Spanish, whereas more than 6 percent of the world's population is Spanish speaking—there is a major business opportunity for Spanish-language Internet-content entrepreneurs. Because of this brain-drain process, however, Latin America has to compete with Miami for this business. In this competition, Miami-based companies will have advantages in infrastructure and financing, as well as many talented emigrants from Latin America to draw on. (See Treverton and Mizell, 2001, p. xix.)

[33]Treverton and Mizell (2001) give data regarding the digital divide in Mexico and elsewhere in Latin America.

[34]The Latin American nations need external investment capital to prosper and grow. But instabilities in these external investment flows have in the past decade caused many problems. (See The Economist, 2002d, for a recent assessment of this situation.)

[35]Argentina is the latest casualty of one of these crises, with unemployment now at 20 percent, more than half of the population living below the official poverty line, the life savings of the Argentine middle class destroyed, hunger and malnutrition emerging in the rural interior, and per capita income declining from $8,909 in 1999 (double that of Mexico and three times that of Poland) to $2,500 in 2002 (roughly on a par with Jamaica and Belarus). (See Faiola, 2002, for a recent update on the situation in Argentina.)

[36]This was the assessment of the experts participating in RAND's November 2000 conference on the information revolution in Latin America. (See Treverton and Mizell, 2001.)

[37]Latin America did not close economic and social gaps during the industrial revolution. It was the assessment of the experts participating in RAND's November 2000 conference on the information revolution in Latin America that the region is unlikely to do so during the information revolution as well. (See Treverton and Mizell, pp. 15, 42.)

[38]Chile could do particularly well if the current negotiations between it and the United States result in a free trade agreement between these two nations.

[39]Faiola (2002) describes the depths of the current financial and social crisis in Argentina.

[40]*The Economist* (2002d) discusses the current financial situation in Brazil and Uruguay.

[41]Ernest Wilson introduced the "information revolutionaries" concept at RAND's November 2000 conference on the information revolution in Latin America. (See Treverton and Mizell, 2001, pp. 23–25.) A more detailed presentation of the theory underlying this concept and its application in specific nations is contained in Wilson (2003).

FEW MIDDLE EASTERN AND NORTH AFRICAN NATIONS WILL FULLY EXPERIENCE THE INFORMATION REVOLUTION, SOME MAY MISS IT ALTOGETHER

The Middle East was once home to the world's most advanced societies, skilled at mathematics, astronomy, science, and medicine, and renowned for their poetry and arts. This coincided roughly with the maximum extent of the Islamic empire, the remnants of which today—with the exception of Turkey—are lumped together as the Middle East and North Africa (MENA), as listed in Table 11.1.[1]

Many of these MENA nations—with the prominent exception of Israel—may miss the information revolution entirely, causing this region to fall even farther behind OECD nations.[2]

IT PENETRATION IS GENERALLY LOW IN MOST MENA NATIONS

With a few notable exceptions, IT penetration is low (i.e., below world averages) in most MENA nations.[3] The exceptions (with penetration well above world averages in 2001) are Bahrain, Israel, and the United Arab Emirates (UAE) for telephones; Bahrain, Israel, Kuwait, Qatar, and the UAE for PCs; and Bahrain, Israel, Kuwait, and the UAE for Internet users. Although often thought of as a wealthy, well-endowed nation, Saudi Arabia was well below world averages in numbers of telephones, PCs, and Internet users in 2001, as were most of the other MENA nations.[4] Yemen, by far the poorest MENA nation and the only one classed as one of the world's "least developed countries" by the United Nations, has IT penetration numbers that rival the poorest nations anywhere in the world.[5]

Table 11.1

Countries of the Middle East and North Africa

The Middle East		
Levant	Arabian Peninsula	
Israel	Bahrain	Saudi Arabia
Jordan	Kuwait	United Arab Emirates
Lebanon	Oman	Yemen
Syria	Qatar	
The Persian Gulf		
Iran, Iraq, and six Arabian Peninsula countries bordering the Gulf		
North Africa		
Maghreb	Mashriq	
Algeria	Egypt	
Morocco	Libya	
Tunisia		

Moreover, irrespective of its magnitude, the pattern of IT diffusion and use in the region is irregular, favoring the wealthy and privileged. This could increase the economic and social disparities between the richest and poorest sectors of MENA societies as time goes on.[6]

MENA NATIONS CAN BE GROUPED INTO THREE CATEGORIES REGARDING THE INFORMATION REVOLUTION

None of the region's governments, except for Israel, has been installed as the result of what the United States considers "free and fair" elections. To compensate for the absence of a popular mandate, these governments maintain strong central control over most aspects of life and commerce.[7]

Control of information flows is central to maintaining control over the populace in the MENA nations—again, except for Israel—and is also central to commercial practices. So, technology that speeds and broadens the dissemination of information can be counter to the government's needs. As each new information technology (e.g., telephone, radio, television) appeared in the past, however, the authorities came to terms with it and adapted the technology to their own purposes.[8] So, too, the MENA governments are coming to terms with the Internet; but because this technology is more complicated than its predecessors, it is more difficult to harness effectively while at the same time limiting "inappropriate" uses.[9] But that has not stopped any government in the region from trying.

Their attempts fall into three categories: those MENA nations that are "fearful," those that are "driven," and those desiring the "best of both."[10]

The "Fearful" Nations

The fearful MENA nations include Algeria, Iraq, Libya, and Syria, countries that have limited Internet connectivity or have prohibited it altogether. They would rather forgo the potential benefits to ensure that they avoid any negative consequences of joining the networked world.[11]

The "Best of Both" Nations

The "best of both" nations are Iran, Saudi Arabia, Tunisia, and the UAE, each of which has tried to develop a tightly controlled domestic Internet network that will enable it to reap benefits in commerce, academia, and government while keeping a close watch and maintaining strict limits on what can and cannot be done and what kinds of information are available.[12] Iran and Tunisia rely largely on regulatory measures, while Saudi Arabia and the UAE have, predictably, spent vast fortunes on technical solutions. None is foolproof, but the governments seem satisfied that their respective solutions ameliorate the dangers acceptably.[13]

The "Driven" Nations

The rest of the MENA nations can be characterized as "driven." They want what the information revolution offers, and want it badly enough to be willing to risk some disbenefits that may arise from more open and possibly "unacceptable" communications.[14] The wealthy countries, including Bahrain, Kuwait, and Qatar, have well-developed information infrastructures. The poorest country, Yemen, has achieved very little. The middle-tier countries (Egypt, Jordan, Lebanon, Morocco, and Oman) have made interesting but unexceptional progress. Commercial relationships and personal influence are as important in these latter countries as the availability of investment funds.[15]

THE SOCIAL IMPLICATIONS OF THE INFORMATION REVOLUTION FOR THE MENA NATIONS COULD BE WIDE-RANGING

The social implications of these developments are potentially wide-ranging, particularly regarding the impact of global social familiarization and changes in the status of women.[16]

Global social familiarization is proceeding quickly in the MENA region, enabled primarily by the rapid proliferation of Arabic- (and also Farsi-) language satellite television transmission and reception over the past decade. This has given the MENA populations their first extensive look at Western (and other non-MENA) culture.[17] This competition between Western and traditional cultures, particularly as they appeal to the young, is causing many people to feel that the continued vitality and possibly even long-term existence of their national (i.e., Arab/Islamic) cultures may be threatened.

Regarding the status of women, traditional mores are being challenged in all these countries as there are increasing demands for women to be more openly integrated into public life.[18] The potential for information and communications technologies to empower women through better education, less-constrained communications, and the ability to generate their own incomes should not be underestimated.[19] A new class of "information workers," likely to be largely female, could emerge over time as a result of IT-related developments. This would have enormous social implications.[20]

FEW MENA NATIONS WILL FULLY EXPLOIT THE INFORMATION REVOLUTION, CAUSING THIS REGION TO FALL EVEN FURTHER BEHIND OECD NATIONS

With the exception of Israel, which we discuss separately below, only a few MENA nations—principally Bahrain, Kuwait, Qatar, and the

UAE—are likely to fully exploit opportunities offered by the information revolution. Most of the others will lag behind, because of inadequate physical infrastructures and human capital, governmental policies that hinder development, or cultural impediments, causing this region to fall even further behind the OECD nations.[21]

The "Driven" Nations

The information revolution future for the "driven" countries promises more of the same, with each investing as much as it can and growing as rapidly as possible in order to achieve the full benefits of IT. The principal limiting factor will be money, but in many countries the Internet has proliferated widely enough to begin providing economic benefits significantly greater than the required investment. Private-sector investment will be the principal source of capital in most nations, although public-sector financing will remain important in Jordan, with a relatively weaker economy than the others, and in Kuwait, for supporting the educational sector.

Some driven nations will do better than others. Bahrain, Kuwait, and Qatar will continue to make the most progress toward information-centric futures as they seek to replace oil revenues that will decrease over time with other intangible products befitting their small size and lack of industrial base.[22]

Jordan and Morocco will probably continue modernizing their IT infrastructures and perhaps enjoy some economic resurgence as a result but are unlikely to achieve anything particularly noteworthy insofar as the information revolution is concerned. The same is true of Egypt.[23]

In IT as in other areas, Oman is likely to continue on the slow, well-considered and well-controlled growth path that it has been on over the past 30 years. This will leave Oman somewhat of a backwater, IT-wise, as it is today.[24]

Lebanon is likely to achieve significant IT-related (and more broadly, economic) growth sporadically at best, as the government's attempts to control information flows and the media wax and wane, and as long as Syria's occupation of a portion of the country continues. Also, the Lebanese economy's significant and lasting downturn may adversely affect private investment.[25]

That leaves Yemen, by far the poorest nation in the MENA region and one of the poorest in the world. Absent reform, stability, and economic development, Yemen could continue to be a breeding ground for terrorists. This, combined with its lack of physical infrastructure (electricity, telecommunications, etc.)[26] should ensure it a dismal future, information revolution–wise.[27]

The "Best of Both" Nations

Among the "best of both" nations, the UAE should make the most progress toward an information-centric future, while continuing its policy of promoting IT growth on the one hand and enforcing fairly strict censorship on the other.[28]

Continued progress in Iran and Saudi Arabia insofar as the information revolution is concerned will depend on how well these regimes manage the popular pressures growing in both of these nations. The Iranian government's schizophrenic attempts to grow but control the Internet reflect the government's larger divisions between the "moderates" or "reformers" and the "hard-liners."[29] How this division plays out—and how long it takes to play out—remains to be seen.

Although the Saudi government has declared IT development to "be a centerpiece of national policy,"[30] access to the Internet remains strictly controlled by the state, which maintains the only international gateway.[31] The requirement to connect to this single, government-owned gateway using the government-owned telecommunications network allows the Saudi government to keep Internet access costs quite high relative to the income of an average citizen. As long as this policy continues, IT-related growth and innovation in Saudi Arabia will lag behind other leading nations in the region (e.g., Bahrain, Kuwait, Qatar, the UAE).[32]

Tunisia will probably continue on as it has in recent years, slowly and unspectacularly.[33]

The "Fearful" Nations

The possible IT-related futures of the "fearful" countries are quite varied, and it is not possible to predict with any degree of reliability how they might play out. It is possible, however, to describe the limiting factors and the probable outcomes of any changes in them.

In Algeria, it is possible that the level of domestic violence and the regime's repressive responses will diminish over time. If this happens, the economy will start to grow again, albeit slowly, in IT-related and other areas.[34]

The prospects for any development (IT-related or otherwise) in Iraq are bleak as long as the regime of Saddam Hussein remains in power.[35] If and when there is a regime change—due to current U.S. efforts or other events—the nature of any successor regime will critically determine Iraq's future course.[36] Given where Iraq is today, it should take it a long time to catch up in the information revolution, even in the best of (post-Saddam) circumstances.

Libya, however, appears to be emerging, slowly, from its exile from the world community, initially self-imposed but reinforced by international sanctions in response to Libya's support for terrorism.[37] It is possible that the Al Qadhafi regime will continue to carefully loosen restrictions on commerce and Internet connectivity in an effort to boost foreign trade and hard currency earnings.[38]

Syria is also emerging from self-imposed isolation, although its continued occupation of Lebanon and the lack of a regional peace settlement will continue to hinder foreign investment and cause the government security headaches. The "informatization" of Syrian society has been championed by the new president and spearheaded by the Syrian Computer Society, two senior members of which were recently appointed to ministerial positions. The government is not so concerned about restricting access to particular sources of information or entertainment as it is about limiting and monitoring the communications resources potentially available to the regime's many enemies.[39]

Israel

As with most everything else in the MENA region, Israel is a special case insofar as the information revolution is concerned. In early 2000, before the current intifada started, it ranked third in the world in the number of NASDAQ-listed companies.[40] During the latter half of the 1990s, Israel developed a venture capital industry, with investment capital flowing into the country from elsewhere in the world, particularly the United States. As a result, in 2000 the number of Israeli startup firms per capita was the highest anywhere in the world except for Silicon Valley.[41] This led to Israeli strengths in a number of IT areas, including Internet telephony, an industry largely erected upon Israeli innovations.[42] These were among Israel's strengths in 2000. Since then, the intifada has put all this at risk. Clearly, Israel's future as a world player in the information revolution is held at least partially hostage to the outcome of the Arab-Israeli peace process.[43,44]

NOTES

[1]Although a country of Muslims, Turkey is not an Islamic state by any metric; it is officially and aggressively secular. While Turkey shares in some of the information revolution concerns of the MENA region, its development process and prospects are unique and merit detailed examination separately. It is not considered further in this chapter.

[2]The chapter draws heavily on the data, analysis, and findings presented in Burkhart and Older (2003). As pointed out there, Israel is generally an exception to MENA norms; it can almost be said not to be a Middle Eastern country except for geography. Accordingly, we discuss Israel separately at the end of this chapter.

[3]The International Telecommunications Union (ITU, 2001, as reported in Burkhart and Older, 2003) gives the following compilation of IT penetration indicators for the MENA nations:

	Telephones per 100 Inhabitants	PCs per 100 Inhabitants	Internet Users per 10,000 Inhabitants
Algeria	6.36	0.71	19.27
Bahrain	67.15	14.18	1,988.65
Egypt	14.63	1.55	92.95
Iran	18.70	6.97	62.29
Iraq	na	na	na
Israel	128.46	24.59	2,304.86

	Telephones per 100 Inhabitants	PCs per 100 Inhabitants	Internet Users per 10,000 Inhabitants
Jordan	27.12	3.28	409.11
Kuwait	48.79	13.19	1,014.71
Lebanon	40.74	5.62	858.00
Libya	11.83	na	35.84
Morocco	19.60	1.31	131.45
Oman	21.34	3.24	457.49
Palestine	16.82	na	181.21
Qatar	56.76	16.39	655.74
Saudi Arabia	25.81	6.27	134.40
Syria	12.09	1.63	36.12
Tunisia	14.90	2.37	412.37
United Arab Emirates	111.66	15.83	3,392.39
Yemen	3.01	0.19	8.89
United States	110.87	62.25	4,995.10
World Averages	32.77	8.42	823.24

Table—continued

na = not available.

[4]According to Burkhart and Older (2003), the most widespread IT presence throughout the MENA nations is television, spurred on by the proliferation of Ku-band satellite television channels that can be received by small and relatively inexpensive—even in the poorest countries—antennas. Every government in the region has established at least one national satellite television channel, in part to spread its message throughout its own population but also to compete with neighboring countries; *Al-Jazeera*, based in Qatar, is the best known of these. In addition, a number of offshore satellite television channels based in London or elsewhere in Europe also serve the MENA region.

[5]See UNDP (2001).

[6]See Burkhart and Older (2003).

[7]Besides being necessary from the government's point of view, rule by a strong central leader or group is a cultural norm in most of these societies. (See Burkhart and Older, 2003.)

[8]For example, telephones not only allowed people to talk to one another at a distance but also provided the government the potential to listen in on conversations that might otherwise have taken place in person, which is less susceptible to eavesdropping. Similarly, radio and television became propaganda and socialization tools in the MENA nations. (See Burkhart and Older, 2003.)

[9]The definition of "inappropriate" has usually included antigovernment and porno-graphic information. Countries with strong Islamic leadership, such as Saudi Arabia, also prohibit access to information denigrating Islam or extolling or proselytizing for other religions. (See Burkhart and Older, 2003.)

[10]Burkhart and Older (2003) created these three categories. Much of what follows is drawn from them.

[11]Syria recently made some cautious steps toward the Internet, and Libya is testing the waters also. See Burkhart and Older (2003) for more details regarding these nations.

[12]Today the UAE is among the leaders in the MENA region in IT penetration and usage. Iran, Saudi Arabia, and Tunisia all lag well behind. (See endnote 3.)

[13]See Burkhart and Older (2003) for more details regarding these nations.

[14]The information revolution is occurring at a time when the MENA nations are suffering from rapid population growth and economic stagnation. The job markets have not kept pace at all with the increasing numbers of young people entering them, leading to increased social tensions. The governments and commercial sectors of the "driven" countries in particular understand that the information revolution can create jobs, revive local economies, and help ameliorate this situation. (See Burkhart and Older, 2003.)

[15]Again, see Burkhart and Older (2003) for more details.

[16]See Burkhart and Older (2003) for further discussion of the social implications of the information revolution for the MENA nations.

[17]The elites in the MENA region have been exposed to Western culture for many years. Only recently has this exposure spread to the bulk of the population. (See Burkhart and Older, 2003.)

[18]The current status of women in Arab nations, the advances they have made in recent years, and the long way they still have to go in most Arab nations are discussed in the *Arab Human Development Report* (AHDR) recently issued by the United Nations. (See UNDP, 2002.)

[19]Trofimov (2002) presents a recent picture of how the status of women is improving in Qatar, which until 1995 was one of the most culturally conservative MENA nations.

[20]Burkhart and Older (2003) discuss the possible emergence of a new class of female information workers in the MENA region in more detail.

[21]According to the AHDR, the MENA region's lagging participation in the information revolution is likely to result in a major brain drain. The AHDR found that 51 percent of all adolescents and 45 percent of preteens expressed a desire to leave the MENA region altogether—presumably for the Western world. (See UNDP, 2002, and Hunaidi, 2002.)

[22]The IT infrastructures in Bahrain, Kuwait, and Qatar will fully meet demand within the next five years, although the degree of Internet use will depend on the pricing poli-

cies of the public sector–dominated Internet service providers. (See Burkhart and Older, 2003.)

[23]Jordan and Morocco do not contribute significantly to regional politics or economy, so whether or not they do well in the information revolution is of little consequence. Egypt is quite different, however. Its continued IT development is critical for economic expansion and continued social stability, which is in turn critical for regional peace. (See Burkhart and Older, 2003. In their words, "Egypt's disaffected cannot all be arrested and won't stay at home forever.")

[24]See Burkhart and Older (2003) for further discussion of Oman.

[25]See Burkhart and Older (2003).

[26]The infrastructure in Yemen in general is so poorly developed and unreliable that the late editor of the *Yemen Times* speculated that the principal impediment to the spread of information technology was the lack of reliable electrical power. (Goodman et al., 1998, as reported in Burkhart and Older, 2003.)

[27]See Burkhart and Older (2003) for further discussion of Yemen's IT situation and prospects.

[28]According to Burkhart and Older (2003), the government of the UAE has thus far been able to blunt public criticism by continued investment aimed at keeping network growth in line with demand. As long as the general public in the UAE can do what it wants for the most part and the Internet-related services are relatively rapid, the public does not seem to mind censorship too much. And, also according to Burkhart and Older, those who do mind seem adept at finding ways around the censorship.

[29]Iran's security and religious watchdogs clearly seek tighter controls and more limited access, while the educational and private sectors are attempting to achieve the opposite, and the public at large—that segment of the public that has the education and means potentially to use the Internet—is generally in favor of unrestricted access. (See Burkhart and Older, 2003.)

[30]See Kashkoul and Ba-Isa (2002).

[31]This gateway is heavily guarded by multiple, redundant firewalls in what must be the most complex and expensive attempt at content filtering in the world. (See Burkhart and Older, 2003, for more details.)

[32]See Burkhart and Older (2003).

[33]According to Burkhart and Older (2003), internal pressures in Tunisia are unlikely to grow significantly, the prospects for "business as usual" are good, and the regime's policy toward the Internet should generally reflect the degree of tension between the government and citizenry at any given time.

[34]Algeria caught the first wave of the information revolution, but further development was quickly curtailed by the government in the face of domestic terrorism and open insurrection. Economic stagnation and the lack of pluralism fed extremist responses that were answered in kind by the regime, generating an economic downturn and tighter government controls. (See Burkhart and Older, 2003.)

[35]Saddam's control of the media and other information sources has been nearly as absolute as Kim Jong-il's grip on North Korea, allowing the government to propagate its own version of recent history and current events. The information infrastructure within Iraq and between Iraq and the outside world has been virtually eliminated. Only parts of the northern Kurdish regions have less restricted access to the outside world, but these areas have other problems that also preclude any IT-related progress. (See Burkhart and Older, 2003.)

[36]These words were written in late 2002, before the war in Iraq.

[37]Despite the sanctions, Libya purchased and commissioned its first digital cellular telephone network in the mid-1990s. Its attempt to commercialize that company, however, failed, as did a faltering attempt to privatize the state telecommunications monopoly. Although Libya has oil income, it is not well distributed and the bulk has been spent on a massive water distribution project spanning more than a decade—with little left for IT-related investment. (See Burkhart and Older, 2003.)

[38]Although there have been several minor insurrections in recent years, the Libyan government faces no organized resistance and appears to understand that the best path to continued domestic peace lies in economic development, which, in turn, relies on trade and foreign investment. (See Burkhart and Older, 2003.)

[39]See Burkhart and Older (2003).

[40]See Hiltzik (2000).

[41]According to Lipschultz (2000þ), in 2000 most of these Israeli high-tech firms had only their corporate headquarters and research and development operations located in Israel, with the majority of their operations (marketing, manufacturing, distribution, etc.) based outside the country.

[42]Hiltzik (2000), Lipschultz (2000a), and Sugarman (2000) discuss these and other aspects of Israel's IT industry.

[43]Opinions differ regarding how fragile Israel's high-tech industry is. According to Hiltzik (2000), while with continued peace Israel's emerging high-tech industry is likely to stay, prosper, and grow, without peace, or even worse, with the reemergence of conflict, much of this industry will leave Israel, going elsewhere in the world (primarily to the United States). However, Lipschultz (2000b) finds Israel's high-tech industry to be much more robust, with no companies likely to leave in the absence of full-scale war. (How close the events of the past two years come to "full-scale war" is another question.)

[44]Israel's information revolution (and more broadly, economic) future may also be hampered by its large and growing number of Arab citizens who represent a significant underclass unlikely to make much progress in the near term. (See Burkhart and Older, 2003.)

MOST COUNTRIES OF SUB-SAHARAN AFRICA WILL FALL FURTHER BEHIND IN THE INFORMATION REVOLUTION

THERE ARE EXTREME DISPARITIES AMONG AFRICAN NATIONS; AS A RESULT, FEW STATEMENTS APPLY UNIVERSALLY

The African continent is extremely diverse, and few blanket statements can be made about information technology and information revolution developments that apply to the continent as a whole. We concentrate here on sub-Saharan Africa, but any statistics or recommendations must take into account the fact that South Africa overwhelms most statistical statements or projections for that region.

As one example of these disparities, South Africa has roughly half of the continent's IT infrastructure. North Africa and Nigeria each have about one-sixth, and all the rest of Africa accounts for only one-sixth of the infrastructure.[1] Even excluding South Africa, there are also dramatic disparities among the northern, eastern, western, and southern African regions, and within countries of those regions.

IN AFRICA, MASS MEDIA PREDOMINATE OVER POINT-TO-POINT COMMUNICATION

With those caveats, there are several measures that help place Africa in context. First, mass media (radio, television) are now, and will remain for the next decade or so at least, the predominant information dissemination media in Africa. For every telephone in Africa, there are 2,500 televisions and 14,000 radios.[2]

COMPARED WITH THE REST OF THE WORLD, AFRICA IS FALLING BEHIND

In 1990, Africa had 2 percent of the world's telephones, but in 2000 it had only 0.8 percent. (These data, taken from International Tele-communications Union tables, represent fixed lines, not wireless, and there are now more mobile telephone subscribers in Africa than fixed-line subscribers.[3] Nevertheless, with about 12 percent of the world's population, Africa is far behind in per capita telephone subscribers.)

Regarding Internet access, South Africa again dominates the continent's usage; it has approximately 750,000 dial-up Internet subscribers out of about 1.36 million for all of Africa, or about 55 percent of the total. The 10 countries of Central Africa,[4] by comparison, have a combined total of just 10,000 subscribers (1.4 percent of Africa's total).[5] Overall, in 1998, Africa had just 4 percent of the world's Internet hosts[6] and 0.22 percent of World Wide Web sites.[7]

One must also remember how poor Africa is in general. At an earlier conference in the RAND/NIC series on the global course of the information revolution, one speaker commented that the wealthiest 15 individuals in the world, taken together, have a greater net worth than all of sub-Saharan Africa.[8]

AFRICA'S IT PROBLEMS ARE NOT PRIMARILY TECHNICAL: THEY INVOLVE FACTORS OF CULTURE, COMPETENCE, CAPITAL, AND CONTROL

Many factors shape a nation's approach to the information revolution, such as GDP per capita, how a society deals with change, the role of government and laws, and the structure of capital markets.[9] These factors, of course, are relevant to the nations of Africa too; however, even more fundamental factors seem to apply in Africa, so we use a "four Cs" categorization to introduce and discuss those factors: culture, competence, capital, and control.[10] We describe those categories below and relate them to selected examples within sub-Saharan Africa.

Cultural Factors Complicate and Impede the Spread and Use of Information Technology in Africa

Cultural factors such as language, nationalism, stratification, legal framework, vertical authority relationships, trust, meritocracy, and concept of information complicate and impede the spread and use of information technology in Africa. For example, if the predominant language of the country is not one of the world's most prominent, many of the world's websites will be unreadable, and software will be late in being translated into that language (if at all). Consider the case of the Democratic Republic of the Congo. Some 200 to 250 dialects are spoken, with Swahili, Lingaga, Tshiluba, and Kikongo as officially recognized national languages. However, some of the young Congolese who have attended the better schools are literate in English.[11] South Africa has 11 official languages, although English might be considered a unifying force in that country. In West Africa particularly, a number of countries use French as their predominant international language, creating a divide of scarce information resources between those tailored for French speakers and those tailored for English speakers.

Another cultural factor is nationalism. If the nation is strongly nationalistic, it will tend to resist "foreign" influences, such as those provided by IT products and services originating elsewhere. A possible negative influence of IT in some African countries is its use by nationalists to spread violent polemics; in the hands of extremists, it could be used for further disruption. This applies both to mass broadcast media and to interactive communications on the Internet and call-in radio. Throughout much of Africa, there are strong ties to tribes that can be reinforced through these media, complicating efforts at regional or continentwide solutions.

Consider various forms of stratification within most African societies. Much of the Internet penetration in Africa is within the major cities, yet most of the population lives in the countryside. In a discussion of Nigeria, for example, it is stated that "80 percent of the people live outside the cities. . . . In the rural areas, travel of 50 km to a pay phone is average."[12] High illiteracy rates also create stratification in use of the Internet, although mass media such as radio can ameliorate this problem.

It Takes an Educated Populace to Know How to Bring IT to Those Who Most Need It

The category of competence involves factors such as education, training, and sophistication of IT use. In sub-Saharan Africa, approximately 23 percent of youth ages 15 to 24 are illiterate (year 2000 figures), and as of 1998 in Central and Western Africa, only 57 percent of children of primary-school age were enrolled in school.[13] The stratification in IT use between educated versus uneducated and urban versus rural is likely to continue into coming generations. Because of these factors, the important role of mass information technologies such as radio and television, rather than the Internet, is also likely to continue in Africa for at least the next decade or two.

Many sub-Saharan Countries Lack Financial and Physical Capital

A third category of factors relevant to IT usage and expansion involves the availability of financial and physical capital, either from within the country or provided by external parties that view the region as a good investment. Physical capital includes the installed base of electric power and telecommunications: Are they available, stable, and provided at reasonable cost? Many countries in Africa are hampered by the fact that the telecommunication system has been a state monopoly, and the state is reluctant to give up this important source of revenue. License fees for alternative telecommunication services have therefore remained prohibitively high: In Nigeria, a multioperator license for a voice satellite link (VSAT) costs more than $100,000; to create an Internet Service Provider (ISP) in Zambia, the fee is $40,000.[14] And, as a recent report indicates, in West Africa there is regionalized war that seems intractable and resistant to peace-keeping; that war is a deterrent to investment because spending goes to training the military rather than into IT.[15,16]

Investment *is* being made in telecommunications and Internet infrastructure in Africa, but factors such as the above create impediments that increase the likelihood that Africa will fall further behind much of the rest of the world in IT developments.

The Agencies of Control in sub-Saharan African Countries Often Impede IT Development

Another set of factors influencing IT development involves the exercise of control. It is important to ask of a country: Who has the power to determine and effect the spread of IT within the country? In particular, is control lodged primarily in a government, the military, religious organizations, or the private sector? And is this control restrictive and constraining, or promotional and guiding? While many African countries' regimes were highly centralized and controlling in the past, a recent report indicates that

> [The years 1995–2000] continued the process of policy decentralization. Support for the old statist model weakened. There were significant increases in countries' competitive market orientation in the [IT] marketplace. And where only a few years earlier government had owned virtually all the [IT] sector, now a new amalgamation of foreign, domestic, public, and private ownerships emerged.[17]

In forward-looking countries, there is also increasing reliance on regulatory agencies that are relatively independent of governmental control and that oversee IT developments in a balanced manner. In other countries (Kenya is an often-cited example), central government continues to dictate and restrict IT policy to a degree considered unhealthy for adequate expansion and accessibility to the country's citizens.[18]

THERE ARE, HOWEVER, POSITIVE INDICATIONS THAT THE INFORMATION REVOLUTION IS MOVING FORWARD IN AFRICA

Most of the factors discussed above are impediments to rapid IT growth in Africa. However, substantial progress is being made. There is growth of kiosks, cybercafes, and other forms of public Internet access; PCs are being added to community telephone-access shops and schools; the ISP "Africa Online" has established hundreds of public-access kiosks as part of a franchise program; and cellular telephone usage is expanding dramatically, especially in countries with poor traditional phone service.[19]

Other indicators are also positive: per capita telephone penetration nearly tripled from 0.16 to 0.39 per 100 people between 1996 and 1999, and by 2001 the number of cell phones will equal 80 percent of the 1996 landline telephone density;[20] and the number of television and radio broadcasters has increased to include private owners, domestic content, and continental coverage.[21] More than 600 ISPs now exist in Africa, with a total outgoing bandwidth of more than 700 megabits per second.[22]

EXTERNAL FACTORS MAY INDIRECTLY IMPEDE IT GROWTH IN AFRICA

Two additional external factors, however, may impede dramatic IT growth in Africa: the HIV/AIDS epidemic, and a refocusing of U.S. attention after the events of September 11, 2001.

The HIV/AIDS Epidemic in Africa Affects the Region's Development Prospects

At the end of 2001, it was estimated that more than 28 million sub-Saharan African adults and children (about 8.4 percent of the population) were infected with HIV/AIDS—of 40 million cases worldwide.[23] Approximately 2.3 million sub-Saharan Africa adults and children died of the disease during 2001. In six sub-Saharan countries, more than 20 percent of all adults ages 15 to 49 have HIV or AIDS,[24] and these cases are affecting the most productive sector of society. These statistics will not improve soon: The vast majority of Africans living with HIV do not know they have acquired the virus. AIDS has become the biggest threat to the continent's development.

In the Post-9/11 Era, Much of the World's Attention and Resources Will Be Focused Elsewhere

The second factor relates to September 11, 2001. U.S. government, and other countries', attention and resources are now focused on the war on terrorism and—to a lesser extent—on the continuing Middle East conflict, and other foreign policy interests may suffer or be redirected. World interest in African development is likely to focus on those regions of great instability or governmental collapse that could become "safe harbors" for terrorist cells. Support for IT-related developments is likely to concentrate on issues of security and governmental stabilization, such as the use of IT for improved airport security.[25]

For all the reasons stated above, it is likely that information technology improvements will continue in Africa, but the region will continue to fall further behind much of the rest of the world during the next several decades.

NOTES

[1]These statistics and much of the rest of the discussion in this chapter are taken from the conference proceedings of the Workshop on Information Technology in Africa (NIC/State Department, 2002). The workshop was held in October 2001 in Washington, D.C.

[2]NIC/State Department (2002), p. 13.

[3]NIC/State Department (2002), p. 19. By comparison, Latin America has 6 percent of the telephone lines and 8 percent of the population, and Asia has 13 percent of the lines and 57 percent of the population. (These statistics are from a white paper distributed at the NIC conference, "An Overview of Internet Connectivity in Africa" by Mike Jensen, August 5, 1998.)

[4]Central Africa comprises Chad, Cameroon, Central African Republic, Gabon, Equatorial Guinea, Sao Tome and Principe, Republic of the Congo, Rwanda, Burundi, and Democratic Republic of the Congo.

[5]NIC/State Department (2002), p. 20.

[6]Jensen, "An Overview of Internet Connectivity in Africa," p. 12.

[7]NIC/State Department (2002), p. 13.

[8]Hundley (2000), p. 54.

[9]Such factors are described in more detail in Chapter Six of this report.

[10]These four factors were introduced by Ernest Wilson at the NIC conference documented in Hundley et al. (2000), and presented for discussion at the NIC Workshop on Information Technology in Africa (NIC/State Department, pp. 10–11). The discussion in this section is adapted from the reports of those two conferences.

[11]NIC/State Department (2002), p. 36.

[12]NIC/State Department (2002), p. 44.

[13]United Nations Economic and Social Council figures, available at http://www. africana.com/Articles/tt_215.htm (accessed by the authors during the course of their research).

[14]NIC/State Department (2002), pp. 45, 51.

[15]NIC/State Department (2002), p. 49.

[16]West Africa comprises the countries of Mauritania, Mali, Niger, Nigeria, Benin, Togo, Ghana, Cote d'Ivoire, Liberia, Sierra Leone, Guinea, Guinea-Bissau, Senegal, Cape Verde, and Burkina Faso

[17]Ernest Wilson III and Kelvin Wong, "African Information Revolution: A Balance Sheet," white paper distributed at NIC Workshop on Information Technology in Africa (unpublished).

[18]Wilson and Wong, "African Information Revolution: A Balance Sheet."

[19]Mike Jensen, "The African Internet: A Status Report," white paper distributed at NIC Workshop on Information Technology in Africa (unpublished).

[20]Wilson and Wong, "African Information Revolution: A Balance Sheet."

[21]Wilson and Wong, "African Information Revolution: A Balance Sheet."

[22]NIC/State Department (2002), p. 20.

[23]Joint United Nations Programme on HIV/AIDS, "AIDS Epidemic Update," December 2001. Available at http://www.unaids.org/epidemic_update/report_dec01/index. html (accessed April 15, 2003). All the statistics and statements in this paragraph are taken from this report.

[24]Sub-Saharan countries with over 20 percent infection rates are Botswana (38.8 percent), Namibia (22.5 percent), South Africa (20.1 percent), Swaziland (33.4 percent), Zambia (21.5 percent), and Zimbabwe (33.7 percent). Taken from the UNAIDS "Report on the Global HIV/AIDS Epidemic" (July 2002). See http://www.avert.org/subaadults. htm (accessed April 15, 2003).

[25]NIC/State Department (2002), pp. 53–54.

PART III. SOME ADDITIONAL TOPICS (A BRIEF LOOK)

GEOPOLITICAL TRENDS FURTHERED BY THE INFORMATION REVOLUTION COULD POSE CONTINUING CHALLENGES TO THE UNITED STATES

In this chapter, we take a brief look at these trends—meant merely to introduce the subject to the reader.

THE U.S. ECONOMY AND SOCIETY ARE WELL POISED TO MEET THE CHALLENGES OF THE INFORMATION REVOLUTION

The economies, societies, and polities that will flourish in the information revolution are those most adept at dealing with change.[1] The United States is best positioned (among all nations) to do well in this new world.[2] Among other things, the information revolution will continue to enhance U.S. soft power.[3]

THERE ARE LIKELY TO BE MANY LOSERS OR LAGGARDS ELSEWHERE IN THE WORLD, SOME OF WHOM COULD BECOME SERIOUSLY DISAFFECTED

Some nations or societies will fall behind in the information revolution because they are too rigid.[4] Other nations or societies will fall behind because they lack the necessary physical, human, financial, and/or institutional capital.[5] Still other nations or societies will fall behind for other reasons. Many of these losers or laggards will become disaffected—some seriously.

THE INFORMATION REVOLUTION BETTER ENABLES DISAFFECTED PEOPLES TO COMBINE AND ORGANIZE, THEREBY RENDERING THEM POWERS THAT MUST BE DEALT WITH

The information revolution is giving voice to people who previously had little voice and is reaching people who previously were not being reached. This better enables disaffected peoples to combine and organize, thereby rendering them powers that must be dealt with—in many, but not all, cases.[6]

THE EXISTENCE OF THESE DISAFFECTED (AND ORGANIZED) LOSERS OR LAGGARDS COULD LEAD TO TRENDS IN THE WORLD THAT MAY CHALLENGE VITAL U.S. INTERESTS

There are many possibilities here. We mention three:

Extreme Losers in the Information Revolution Could Become "Failed States"

Such failed states could become a breeding ground for terrorists, who could threaten vital U.S. interests. This could happen, for example, to some nations in Africa, Latin America, or the Middle East.[7]

Responding to the Information Revolution Will Stress European Economies, Societies, and Polities, Leading to Laggards and Losers Within Europe[8]

This could over time put increased stress on the North Atlantic Alliance, thereby threatening a vital interest of the United States—i.e., that the United States and Europe remain steadfast allies.

The Inability of Japan to Change Sufficiently to Cope with the Information Revolution—If This Turns Out to Be the Case— Could Lead to the Failure of the Japanese Economy

Much has been written in recent years regarding the rigidities of the Japanese society, economy, and government; the difficulties this causes Japan in coping with rapid, profound change, such as that brought on by globalization and the information revolution; and the resulting stagnation of the Japanese economy in recent years.[9] If this condition, which has been pronounced throughout the 1990s, persists, it could lead Japan to fall even further behind the nations in the vanguard of the information revolution and, in the extreme, could lead to the failure of the Japanese economy.[10,11]

The failure of Japan's economy would in turn lead to a vacuum in Asia likely to be filled by China. This would greatly enhance China's position within Asia and make it more likely that China becomes a peer competitor of the United States.

THESE TRENDS WOULD POSE CONTINUING CHALLENGES TO U.S. INTERESTS

Increased breeding grounds for terrorists would exacerbate the war on terrorism. Increased stress on the North Atlantic Alliance, if continued long enough, could drive a wedge between the United States and Europe. These, to say nothing of the rise of China as a peer competitor, would pose continuing challenges to U.S. interests.

None of these have to happen—but some or all of them could happen.

NOTES

[1]Chapter Six of this report highlights the manner in which a society deals with change as one of the major factors shaping a nation's posture vis-à-vis the information revolution.

[2]Chapter Seven enumerates the many advantages the United States possesses in dealing with the challenges posed by the information revolution.

[3]*Soft power*, as defined by Keohane and Nye (1998), is "the ability to get desired outcomes because others want what you want." See this article for a discussion of soft

power, why it is important in the information age, and why the information revolution should continue to enhance U.S. soft power.

[4]Several nations in the Middle East and North Africa fall in this category. (See Chapter Eleven.)

[5]A number of nations in Asia, Latin America, the Middle East and North Africa, and sub-Saharan Africa lack one or more of these essential resources. They are discussed in Chapters Nine through Twelve of this report.

[6]Arquilla and Ronfeldt (2001) discuss several recent manifestations of this phenomenon—the empowerment of disaffected peoples.

[7]By "failed state," we mean a government that is unable to exercise effective control within its territorial domain.

[8]Chapter Eight discusses the approach that Europe is taking to the information revolution and the stresses it is causing to European society.

[9]As mentioned in Chapter Nine, Grimond (2002) takes a detailed look at "what ails" the Japanese economy, government, and society today; Iritani (2000) provides a briefer version; and Miyashita (1999) specifically discusses how cultural obstacles to individualism, risk-taking, and entrepreneurship in Japan impede the nation's ability to meet the challenges posed by the information revolution.

[10]By "failure" of the Japanese economy we mean a persistent long-term stagnation of the economy, leading to a pronounced decline in Japan's world economic standing—much as happened to Argentina during the 20th century.

[11]On the other hand, as we mentioned in Chapter Nine, some observers have noted a recent emergence of individualism and entrepreneurship in Japan—including Ono and Spindle (2000), who describe a recent stirring of individualism in Japan, depicting it as a response to the nation's long slump during the 1990s; Lily Wu (private communication, 2002), who reports a noticeable emergence of entrepreneurship in the Japanese IT industry since 2000; and Grimond (2002), who mentions stirrings of individualism among the young in Japan. If this nascent trend persists and spreads, it would offer hope for the near- to mid-term recovery and long-term vitality of the Japanese economy and put to rest the notions of a failed economy.

Chapter Fourteen

WHAT FUTURE EVENTS COULD CHANGE THESE PROJECTIONS?

What future events could change the projections made in this report? Regarding the precise nature of the economic, social, and governmental transformations driven by the information revolution: many things. Regarding the pace of these transformations: many things as well. Regarding the relative performance of various regions of the world: some things. Regarding the degree to which IT ultimately changes the 21st-century world: few if any things.

FUTURE "KILLER APPS," UNCLEAR AT PRESENT, WILL DETERMINE THE PRECISE NATURE OF IT-DRIVEN TRANSFORMATIONS

The details of the economic, social, and governmental transformations driven by the information revolution that occur in coming years depend on the nature of the new IT-enabled products and services that achieve widespread use in business, government, and society. What these products and services will be depends on market forces. In many cases, these markets will be shaped by "killer applications," or "killer apps"—new, revolutionary products or services that create new markets where none existed before.[1] It is difficult to predict when and where future killer apps will emerge; most of the killer apps that emerged in the past were unanticipated, and many of the "predicted" killer apps failed to capture widespread markets. Such killer apps are the wild cards along the future course of the information revolution that will determine the fine details of this revolution.

MANY THINGS CAN SLOW DOWN OR SPEED UP THE PACE OF IT-DRIVEN TRANSFORMATIONS

Adverse financial events can slow down the pace of future IT-driven changes—as the massive overinvestment in telecommunications infrastructures and Internet companies did in the late 1990s. Unexpected killer apps can speed up the pace of future IT-driven changes—as the invention of the World Wide Web and the Netscape browser did in the 1990s.

Such unpredictable events affecting the pace of the information revolution will occur in the future just as they have in the past.

FUTURE GEOPOLITICAL EVENTS COULD ADVERSELY AFFECT HOW DIFFERENT NATIONS AND REGIONS OF THE WORLD FARE

There is one common assumption underlying most of the projections in this report: that neither a new "cold war," nor a global military conflict, nor a large-scale regional conflict will break out in the world over the next 15 to 20 years. If one of those were to happen, it could adversely affect one or more of the regions and/or nations involved—thereby hindering their ability to perform well in the information revolution, possibly substantially. Persistent, widespread, devastating terrorist incidents could have the same effect on a nation or region.

NO MATTER WHAT HAPPENS, THE DEGREE TO WHICH IT ULTIMATELY CHANGES THE WORLD IS UNLIKELY TO CHANGE

Regardless of how future killer apps shape the information revolution, regardless of how future events slow down or speed up the pace of IT-driven transformations, and regardless of whether future geopolitical events adversely affect the course of the information revolution in various regions of the world, the degree to which IT ultimately changes the 21st-century world is unlikely to change. We expect these changes to be profound.

NOTES

[1] Chapter Two of this report discusses the ways in which killer apps can greatly affect markets and create new markets where none existed before.

THE INFORMATION REVOLUTION IS PART OF A BROADER TECHNOLOGY REVOLUTION WITH EVEN PROFOUNDER CONSEQUENCES

The information revolution is not the only technology-driven revolution under way in the world today, merely the most advanced. Advances in biotechnology and nanotechnology, and their synergies with IT, should also change the world greatly over the course of the 21st century.[1]

ADVANCES IN BIOTECHNOLOGY AND NANOTECHNOLOGY WILL ALSO GREATLY CHANGE THE WORLD

Developments in molecular biology since the discovery of the structure and function of DNA in the 1950s have established the knowledge base necessary to profile, copy, and manipulate plant, animal, and human genomes—the genetic basis for life. This enables a wide variety of powerful biotechnology techniques, including gene therapy, for the diagnosis and treatment of disease; designer drugs, tailored to target specific diseases; genetic profiling, to identify those susceptible to specific diseases; genetic identification, to aid in criminal and civil cases; genetically engineered biosensors, for a variety of applications; cloning, to artificially produce genetically identical organisms; and genetically modified organisms, to engineer specific properties into life forms for various reasons (e.g., foods with improved taste, artificially introduced nutrients, or longer shelf life; crops that are resistant to bugs, have in vivo pesticide protection, have greater yield, or grow in previously unproductive environments; and organisms that produce or deliver drugs for human disease control).[2] These powerful techniques will lead to many new products, services, and industries—and will render obsolete many existing products and services. They will revolutionize human health care and make possible major improvements in agriculture. They should have a major impact on the world of the 21st century.[3,4]

Nanotechnology, broadly defined, includes microsystems, nanosystems, and molecular systems.[5] Over the past decade or so, major advances have been made in our ability to understand and control the fundamental building blocks of all physical things, at the micro-, nano-, and molecular levels, making possible integrated microsystems performing a wide variety of tasks, nanofabricated semiconductors that continue Moore's Law to ever smaller scales, molecular manufacturing in which objects are assembled atom by atom (or molecule by molecule) from the bottom up (rather than from the top down using conventional fabrication techniques), and novel nanoscale computers based on molecular electronics or quantum effects, to mention just a few of many possibilities. According to experts in this field, "these developments are likely to change the way almost everything—from vaccines to computers to automobile tires to objects not yet imagined—is designed and made," thereby having a major impact on the 21st-century world.[6]

THERE ARE MANY SYNERGIES BETWEEN IT AND THESE OTHER REVOLUTIONARY TECHNOLOGIES

Advances in information technology have enabled the data processing, storage, and retrieval capabilities necessary to map plant, animal, and human genomes; without these IT capabilities, the revolutionary biotechnology techniques mentioned above would not be feasible.

Likewise, advances in nanotechnology should make possible the continuation of Moore's Law to ever smaller scales, leading to ever-more-powerful computers and memory storage devices of ever-larger capacities.

These are just two of many synergies that exist between information, bio-, and nanotechnologies.[7] As a result of these synergies, the overall economic and societal impact of this combined technology revolution will be even greater than that of the individual technologies.

THE CONSEQUENCES OF THE BIOREVOLUTION WILL BE ESPECIALLY PROFOUND AND QUITE CONTROVERSIAL

The ability to alter plant and animal genomes has already led to considerable controversy; the ability to alter the human genome will lead to enormous controversy.

Genetically modified crops are accepted and in wide use in some parts of the world (e.g., the United States) and rejected in others (e.g., Europe). Restrictions on the free movement of genetically modified crops throughout the world has already become a major international issue.[8] Likewise, the cloning of animals (e.g., "Dolly" the sheep) has become a major controversy in every nation in which it has been attempted.

But these controversies regarding the alteration of plant and animal genomes are nothing compared with the controversies that will arise over attempts to alter the human genome—to use genetic engineering techniques to "improve" the human species and clone humans—because this goes to the very heart of what it means to be "human." As one group of experts who have looked at this issue has said, "This will be a very controversial development, perhaps the most controversial in the history of mankind."[9]

AS WITH THE INFORMATION REVOLUTION, THE BIO- AND NANOREVOLUTIONS WILL PLAY OUT UNEVENLY THROUGHOUT THE WORLD

As time goes on and the revolutionary economic and societal consequences of biotechnology and nanotechnology begin to be realized, most likely at an uneven pace throughout the world, a study similar to this one will be called for, on the global course of the bio- and nanorevolutions and their regional variations.

NOTES

[1]This chapter is meant merely to introduce the reader to the existence and revolutionary potential of this broader technology revolution and provide some introductory references.

[2]This is an incomplete list. Antón, Silberglitt, and Schneider (2001) discuss these various biotechnology capabilities in considerable detail and provide extensive references to the relevant literature.

[3]In the view of Antón, Silberglitt, and Schneider (2001), "whereas the 20th century was dominated by advances in chemistry and physics, the 21st century will be dominated by advances in biotechnology."

[4]Enriquez (2001) presents a detailed vision of the profound economic and societal impact that the biorevolution will have throughout the world.

[5]Microsystems are assembled from micron-scale (i.e., 10^{-6} meter) elements. Nanosystems are assembled from nanometer-scale (i.e., 10^{-9} meter) elements. Molecular systems are assembled from individual molecules.

[6]The quote is from National Nanotechnology Initiative (2000), which discusses the potential of nanotechnology in some detail. Antón, Silberglitt, and Schneider (2001) also discuss nanotechnology in considerable detail and provide extensive references to the relevant literature.

[7]Antón, Silberglitt, and Schneider (2001), Enriquez (2001), and NSF/DOC (2002) provide detailed discussions of the many important synergies between these technologies.

[8]Enriquez (2001) discusses the controversy surrounding genetically modified crops and the significance of their acceptance or rejection for the future economic performance of nations.

[9]The quote is attributed to Antón, Silberglitt, and Schneider (2001), who estimate that we may have such human genetic engineering capabilities by 2015.

PARTICIPANTS IN THE RAND/NIC INFORMATION REVOLUTION CONFERENCES

THE NOVEMBER 1999 CONFERENCE ON SOCIETAL TRENDS DRIVEN BY THE INFORMATION REVOLUTION

Dr. Jon B. Alterman (United States)
Middle East Program Officer, United States Institute of Peace

Professor Kim V. Andersen (Denmark)
Department of Informatics, Copenhagen Business School

Dr. Robert H. Anderson (United States)
Senior Information Scientist and Head,
Information Sciences Group, RAND

Professor Vallampadugai S. Arunachalam (India)
Engineering & Public Policy Department and Robotics Institute,
Carnegie Mellon University

Dr. Tora Kay Bikson (United States)
Senior Behavioral Scientist, RAND

Mr. Taylor Boas (United States)
Carnegie Endowment for International Peace

Professor Paul Bracken (United States)
School of Management, Yale University

Mr. Clinton C. Brooks (United States)
Corporate Knowledge Strategist, National Security Agency

Professor Eric Brousseau (France)
Centre ATOM, Universite de Paris I Pantheon Sorbonne

Professor William Caelli (Australia)
School of Data Communications,
Queensland University of Technology

Mr. Colin Crook (United States)
Senior Fellow, Wharton School;
Former Senior Technology Officer, Citibank

Dr. James Dewar (United States)
Senior Mathematician, RAND

Dr. William Drake (United States)
Senior Associate and Director of the Project on the Information
Revolution and World Politics,
Carnegie Endowment for International Peace

Professor Francis Fukuyama (United States)
Institute of Public Policy, George Mason University

Dr. Lawrence K. Gershwin (United States)
National Intelligence Officer for Science & Technology,
National Intelligence Council

Mr. David C. Gompert (United States)
Vice President, National Security Research Division;
Director, National Defense Research Institute, RAND

Professor Sy Goodman (United States)
University of Arizona, Georgia Tech, and Stanford University

Dr. David Gordon (United States)
National Intelligence Officer for Economics and Global Issues,
National Intelligence Council

Dr. Jerrold Green (United States)
Senior Political Scientist, Director of International Development;
Director, Center for Middle East Public Policy, RAND

Dr. Eugene C. Gritton (United States)
Director, Acquisition and Technology Policy Program, RAND

Dr. Richard O. Hundley (United States)
Senior Physical Scientist, RAND

Dr. Paul Kozemchak (United States)
Special Assistant to the Director,
Defense Advanced Research Projects Agency

Dr. John Kriese (United States)
Chief Scientist, Defense Intelligence Agency

Ms. Ellen Laipson (United States)
Vice Chairman, National Intelligence Council

Dr. Martin Libicki (United States)
Senior Policy Analyst, RAND

Mr. John Mabberley (United Kingdom)
Managing Director, DERAtec,
Defence Evaluation and Research Agency

Ms. Yuko Maeda (Japan)
Nomura Research Institute America

Professor Mark Mason (United States)
School of Foreign Service, Georgetown University

Mr. Hideo Miyashita (Japan)
General Manager, Center for Cyber Communities Initiative,
Nomura Research Institute Ltd.

Dr. James Mulvenon (United States)
Associate Political Scientist, RAND

Dr. C. Richard Neu (United States)
Senior Economist and Associate Director, Project Air Force, RAND

Mr. Yoshiyuki Noguchi (Japan)
President, Nomura Research Institute America

Dr. William Nolte (United States)
Director, Outreach and Strategic Planning,
National Intelligence Council

Professor M. J. Norton (United Kingdom)
Head of Electronic Business, Institute of Directors

Mr. Ian Pearson (United Kingdom)
Futurologist, British Telecommunications Laboratories

Professor Larry Press (United States)
Chairman, CIS Department,
California State University at Dominguez Hills

Ms. Betsy Quint-Moran (United States)
Strategic Assessments Group, Office of Transnational Issues,
Central Intelligence Agency

Dr. Enid Schoettle (United States)
Special Advisor to the Chairman, National Intelligence Council

Dr. Brian Shaw (United States)
Deputy National Intelligence Officer for Science & Technology,
National Intelligence Council

Professor Ernest Wilson (United States)
Director, Center for International Development and Conflict
Management, University of Maryland at College Park

Mr. Robert Worden (United States)
Federal Research Division, Library of Congress

Ms. Lily Wu (United States)
Former Director, Equity Research, Salomon Smith Barney,
Hong Kong and San Francisco;
Currently Acting CFO, Disappearing Inc. and MovieQ.com

Mr. Boris Zhikharevich (Russia)
Head, Strategic Planning Department, Leontief Centre,
St. Petersburg

THE MAY 2000 CONFERENCE ON THE TECHNOLOGY DRIVERS OF THE INFORMATION REVOLUTION

Dr. Robert H. Anderson (United States)
Senior Information Scientist and Head,
Information Sciences Group, RAND

Dr. Philip Antón (United States)
Senior Computer Scientist, RAND

Professor Vallampadugai S. Arunachalam (India)
Engineering & Public Policy Department and Robotics Institute,
Carnegie Mellon University

Dr. Steven Bankes (United States)
Senior Computer Scientist, RAND

Mr. John Baskin (United States)
Deputy National Intelligence Officer for Economics and
Global Issues,
National Intelligence Council

Mr. Jeffrey Benjamin (United States)
Senior Associate, Booz Allen Hamilton

Dr. Tora Kay Bikson (United States)
Senior Behavioral Scientist, RAND

Dr. Joel Birnbaum (United States)
Chief Scientist, Hewlett-Packard Company

Mr. Maarten Botterman (The Netherlands)
Research Leader, RAND Europe

Professor William J. Caelli (Australia)
School of Data Communications,
Faculty of Information Technology,
Queensland University of Technology, Australia

Dr. Jonathan Caulkins (United States)
Director, Pittsburgh Office, RAND

Mr. Colin Crook (United States)
Senior Fellow, Wharton School;
Former Senior Technology Officer, Citibank

Professor Peter Denning (United States)
Computer Science Department, George Mason University

Dr. James Dewar (United States)
Senior Mathematician and Director, Research Quality Assurance,
RAND

Dr. David Farber (United States)
   Chief Technologist, Federal Communications Commission;
   Professor, University of Pennsylvania

Dr. Robert Frederking (United States)
   Chair, Graduate Programs in Language Technology,
   Carnegie Mellon University

Professor Erol Gelenbe (United States)
   Associate Dean of Engineering & Computer Science
   University of Central Florida

Dr. Lawrence K. Gershwin (United States)
   National Intelligence Officer for Science & Technology
   National Intelligence Council

Dr. Eugene C. Gritton (United States)
   Director, Acquisition and Technology Policy Program, RAND

Mr. Eric Harslem (United States)
   Senior Vice President of Products and Technology Strategy,
   Dell Computer Corporation

Mr. Stanley Heady (United States)
   Executive for Research Alliances, National Security Agency

Dr. Charles M. Herzfeld (United States)
   Independent Consultant

Dr. Richard O. Hundley (United States)
   Senior Physical Scientist, RAND

Mr. James M. Kearns (United States)
   Financial Design Inc.

Dr. Paul Kozemchak (United States)
   Special Assistant, Intelligence Liaison,
   Defense Advanced Research Projects Agency

Dr. John T. Kriese (United States)
   Chief Scientist, Defense Intelligence Agency

Dr. Douglas Lenat (United States)
   President, CYCORP

Mr. David Marvit (United States)
Director, Strategy, Disappearing Inc.

Professor Noel MacDonald (United States)
Department of Mechanical & Environmental Engineering,
University of California at Santa Barbara

Dr. William Mularie (United States)
Director, Information Systems Office,
Defense Advanced Research Projects Agency

Dr. C. Richard Neu (United States)
Senior Economist, RAND

Dr. Edward C. Oliver (United States)
Director, Advanced Scientific Computing Research,
Department of Energy

Professor Raj Reddy (United States)
Herbert A. Simon University Professor,
Carnegie Mellon University

Professor William L. Scherlis (United States)
School of Computer Science, Carnegie Mellon University

Dr. Enid Schoettle (United States)
Special Advisor to the Chairman, National Intelligence Council

Dr. Brian Shaw (United States)
Deputy National Intelligence Officer for Science & Technology,
National Intelligence Council

Professor Mary Shaw (United States)
School of Computer Science, Carnegie Mellon University

Professor Robert Simon (United States)
Department of Computer Science, George Mason University

Dr. Stephen L. Squires (United States)
Special Assistant for Information Technology,
Defense Advanced Research Projects Agency

Mr. Phillip Webb (United Kingdom)
Chief Information Officer,

Defence Evaluation and Research Agency, Farnborough,
United Kingdom

Ms. Lily Wu (United States)
Chief Financial Officer, XLinux Inc.

Mr. Rick E. Yannuzzi (United States)
Senior Deputy National Intelligence Officer for Strategic and
Nuclear Programs,
National Intelligence Council

THE NOVEMBER 2000 CONFERENCE ON THE COURSE OF THE INFORMATION REVOLUTION IN LATIN AMERICA

Dr. Robert H. Anderson (United States)
Senior Information Scientist and Head,
Information Sciences Group, RAND

Mr. Fulton T. Armstrong (United States)
National Intelligence Officer for Latin America,
National Intelligence Council

Mr. Diego Arria (Venezuela)
Chairman, Technology Holdings International;
Former Permanent Representative of Venezuela at the
United Nations

Dr. John Baskin (United States)
Deputy National Intelligence Officer for Economics and
Global Issues,
National Intelligence Council

Dr. Tora Kay Bikson (United States)
Senior Behavioral Scientist, RAND

Professor Antonio Jose Junqueira Botelho (Brazil)
Department of Politics and Sociology,
Pontifical Catholic University of Rio de Janeiro

Mr. Juan Enriquez (Mexico)
Researcher, David Rockefeller Center for Latin American Studies,
Harvard University;

Former CEO of Mexico City's Urban Development Corporation;
Coordinator General of Economic Policy and Chief of Staff to
Mexico's Secretary of State

Dr. Lawrence K. Gershwin (United States)
National Intelligence Officer for Science & Technology,
National Intelligence Council

Dr. David Gordon (United States)
National Intelligence Officer for Economics and Global Issues,
National Intelligence Council

Dr. Eugene C. Gritton (United States)
Director, Acquisition and Technology Policy Program, RAND

Dr. Timothy Heyman (Mexico)
President, Heyman y Asociados, S.C., Mexico City,
Former President, ING Baring Grupo Financiero (Mexico)

Dr. Richard O. Hundley (United States)
Senior Physical Scientist, RAND

Mr. Elliot Maxwell (United States)
Special Advisor to the Secretary of Commerce for the
Digital Economy,
U.S. Department of Commerce

Ms. Lee Mizell (United States)
Doctoral Fellow, RAND Graduate School

Mr. William T. Ortman (United States)
Deputy National Intelligence Officer for Latin America,
National Intelligence Council

Mr. Jonathan Orszag (United States)
Managing Director, Sebago Associates Inc.;
Former Assistant to the Secretary of Commerce;
Director of the Office of Policy and Strategic Planning,
Department of Commerce

Mr. Ricardo Peon (Mexico)
Manager of Telecoms and Internet Investments,

Heyman y Asociados, S.C., Mexico City;
Former Managing Director, Deutsche Bank Mexico

Mr. Danilo Piaggesi (Italy)
Head, Information Technologies for Development Division,
Inter-American Development Bank

Professor Larry Press (United States)
Chairman, CIS Department,
California State University at Dominguez Hills

Dr. Susan Kaufman Purcell (United States)
Vice President, The Council of the Americas, New York City

Dr. Angel Rabasa (United States)
Senior Policy Analyst, RAND

Mr. David Rothkopf (United States)
Chairman and Chief Executive, Intellibridge Corporation;
Former Acting Under Secretary of Commerce for
International Trade;
Deputy Under Secretary of Commerce for International Trade
Policy Development

Mr. Ricardo Setti (Brazil)
Brazilian Journalist; Latin American Business Consultant

Dr. Brian Shaw (United States)
Deputy National Intelligence Officer for Science & Technology,
National Intelligence Council

Mr. Eduardo Talero (United States)
Principal Informatics Specialist and Informatics
Procurement Advisor,
World Bank

Dr. Gregory Treverton (United States)
Senior Consultant, RAND;
Senior Fellow, Pacific Council on International Policy

Ms. Regina K. Vargo (United States)
Deputy Assistant Secretary of Commerce for the

Western Hemisphere,
U.S. Department of Commerce

Mr. Robert A. Vitro (United States)
Intersectoral, Regional and Special Programs,
Information Technology for Development Division,
Inter-American Development Bank

Professor Ernest Wilson (United States)
Director, Center for International Development and Conflict
Management, University of Maryland at College Park

Mr. Robert Worden (United States)
Federal Research Division, Library of Congress

THE APRIL 2001 CONFERENCE ON THE COURSE OF THE INFORMATION REVOLUTION IN EUROPE

Dr. Robert H. Anderson (United States)
Senior Information Scientist and Head,
Information Sciences Group, RAND

Mr. Neil Bailey (United Kingdom)
Managing Director, Empower Dynamics

Dr. Tora Kay Bikson (United States)
Senior Behavioral Scientist, RAND

Dr. Carl Bildt (Sweden)
Special United Nations Envoy for the Balkans;
Former Prime Minister of Sweden;
Member, Advisory Board, RAND Europe

Mr. Daniel Bircher (Switzerland)
Head, Information and Process Security,
Ernst Basler & Partners Ltd.

Mr. Maarten Botterman (The Netherlands)
Program Director,
Information and Communications Technology Policy Research,
RAND Europe

Mr. J. C. Burgelman (Belgium)
SMIT-VUB

Dr. Gabriella Cattaneo (Italy)
Databank Consulting

Dr. Jonathan Cave (United States)
Senior Economist, RAND Europe

Mr. Anders Comstedt (Sweden)
President, Stokab

Ms. Renée Cordes (Belgium)
Freelance Journalist, Brussels

Mr. Ian Culpin (Belgium)
Martech International, Brussels

Ms. Carine Dartiguepeyrou (France)
Consultant, RAND Europe
Formerly of Solving International, Paris

Ms. Kitty de Bruin (The Netherlands)
Director, NT FORUM

Mr. Pol Descamps (Belgium)
Consultant, PTD Partners

Mr. Job Dittberner (United States)
National Intelligence Council

Mr. Bob Ford (United Kingdom)
Senior Research and Development Manager
British Telecommunications

Dr. Lawrence K. Gershwin (United States)
National Intelligence Officer for Science & Technology,
National Intelligence Council

Dr. Eugene C. Gritton (United States)
Director, Acquisition and Technology Policy Program, RAND

Mr. Kurt Haering (Switzerland)
Director, Foundation InfoSurance, Zurich

Dr. Kris Halvorsen (Norway)
Center Director, Solutions and Services Technologies,
Hewlett Packard Laboratories

Professor Dr. Bernhard M. Hämmerli (Switzerland)
Professor of Informatics, Communications and Security,
Applied University of Technology, Lucerne

Dr. Andrej Heinke (Germany)
DaimlerChrysler

Dr. Richard O. Hundley (United States)
Senior Physical Scientist and Manager,
Information Revolution Project, RAND

Col. Eng. Aurelian Ionescu (Romania)
CIO and IT Advisor to State Secretary,
Romania Ministry of National Defense, Bucharest

Dr. Suzanne Jantsch (Germany)
Project Manager, Information Technology Communications, IABG

Dr. Peter Johnston (United Kingdom)
Head of New Methods of Work,
Information Society Directorate-General,
European Commission

Professor Sergei Kapitza (Russia)
Academy of Science, Moscow

Mr. Thomas Koeppel (Switzerland)
Section Head, Service for Analysis and Prevention,
Swiss Federal Office of Police, Bern

Mr. Ivo Kreiliger (Switzerland)
Deputy Intelligence Coordinator,
Assessment and Detection Bureau, Bern

Professor Eddie C. Y. Kuo (Singapore)
Dean, School of Communication Studies,
Nanyang Technological University, Singapore

Mr. David Leevers (United Kingdom)
VERS Associates

Mr. Stephan Libiszewski (Switzerland)
Attaché for IT, Swiss Mission to NATO, Brussels

Dr. Erkki Liikanen (Finland)
Commissioner, Enterprise and Information Society,
European Commission

Professor Arun Mahizhan (Singapore)
Deputy Director, Institute of Policy Studies, Singapore

Dr. Joan Majo (Spain)
Institut Catalan de Tecnologia

Dr. John McGrath (RN retired) (United Kingdom)
Ex Dean, Royal Navy Engineering College, Manadon

Dr. Adrian Mears (United Kingdom)
Technical Director
Defence Evaluation and Research Agency, Farnborough

Mr. Horace Mitchell (United Kingdom)
Founder and CEO, Management Technology Associates

Dr. C. Richard Neu (United States)
Senior Economist, RAND

Dr. Michelle Norgate (Switzerland)
Center for Security Studies and Conflict Research,
Swiss Federal Institute of Technology, Zurich

Sir Michael Palliser (United Kingdom)
Chairman, Advisory Board, RAND Europe;
Former Vice Chairman, Samuel Montagu & Co., London

Dr. Sarah Pearce (United Kingdom)
Parliamentary Office of Science & Technology, London

Mr. Ian Pearson (United Kingdom)
Futurologist, British Telecommunications Laboratories

Dr. Robert Pestel (Germany)
Senior Scientific Officer,
Information Society Directorate-General,
European Commission

Prof. Richard Potter (United Kingdom)
  Defence Evaluation and Research Agency, Farnborough

Dr. Michel Saloff-Coste (France)
  MSC & Partners, Paris

Mr. Maurice Sanciaume (France)
  Government Affairs Manager Europe,
  Agilent Technologies Belgium

Dr. Brian Shaw (United States)
  Deputy National Intelligence Officer for Science & Technology,
  National Intelligence Council

Mr. Mark Stead (United Kingdom)
  Member of the Director General Information Office of the Ministry
  of Defence

Mr. Eddie Stewart (United Kingdom)
  DERA Webmaster,
  Defence Evaluation and Research Agency

Professor Reima Suomi (Finland)
  University of Turku, Finland

Ms. Pamela Taylor (United Kingdom)
  E-Business Policy Advisor,
  Confederation of British Industry

Mr. Tom Tesch (Belgium)
  Technical University of West Flanders,
  Kortrijk, Belgium

Professor Paul Van Binst (Belgium)
  Director, Telematics and Communications Services,
  Free University of Brussels

Mr. Lorenzo Veleri (United Kingdom)
  Policy Analyst, Kings College, London

Mr. Phillip Webb (United Kingdom)
  Chief Information Officer and Chief Knowledge Office,
  Defence Evaluation and Research Agency, Farnborough

Professor Raoul Weiler (Belgium)
University of Louvain

Dr. Walter Widmer (Switzerland)
Head, IT Security Switzerland, UBS

Anderson, Robert H., Tora K. Bikson, Sally Ann Law, and Bridger M. Mitchell, *Universal Access to E-Mail: Feasibility and Societal Implications,* Santa Monica, Calif.: RAND, MR-650-MF, 1995.

Anderson, Robert H., Philip S. Antón, Steven C. Bankes, Tora K. Bikson, Jonathan Caulkins, Peter J. Denning, James A. Dewar, Richard O. Hundley, and C. Richard Neu, *The Global Course of the Information Revolution: Technology Trends—Proceedings of an International Conference,* Santa Monica, Calif.: RAND, CF-157-NIC, 2000.

Antón, Philip S., Richard Silberglitt, and James Schneider, *The Global Technology Revolution: Bio/Nano/Materials Trends and Their Synergies with Information Technology by 2015,* Santa Monica, Calif.: RAND, MR-1307-NIC, 2001.

Applbaum, Arthur Isak, "Failure in the Cybermarketplace of Ideas," in Elaine Ciulla Kamarck and Joseph S. Ney, Jr., eds., *Governance. com: Democracy in the Information Age,* Washington, D.C.: Brookings Institution Press, 2002, pp. 17–31.

Arquilla, John, and David Ronfeldt, eds., *Networks and Netwars: The Future of Terror, Crime, and Militancy,* Santa Monica, Calif.: RAND, MR-1382-OSD, 2001.

Arunachalam, Vallampadugai S., "Bridging the Digital Divide: The Indian Story," presentation at the RAND Conference on the Global Course of the Information Revolution: Political, Economic, and Social Consequences, Washington, D.C., November 16–18, 1999.

Association for Computing Machinery (ACM), "The Global IT Workforce," *Communications of the ACM,* July 2001, Vol. 44, No. 77, 2001, pp. 30–78.

Baker, Stephen, and Mark Clifford, "Tale of a Bubble: How the 3G Fiasco Came Close to Wrecking Europe," *BusinessWeek,* June 3, 2002, pp. 48–51.

Beatty, Perrin, "Canada in North America: Isolation or Integration?" in Peter Hakim and Robert E. Litan, eds., *The Future of North American Integration: Beyond NAFTA,* Washington, D.C.: Brookings Institution Press, 2002.

Bhaskaran, Manu, *China as Potential Superpower: Regional Responses,* Frankfurt am Main, Germany: Deutsche Bank Research, January 15, 2003.

Bikson, Tora K., "The Proximity Paradox: Opportunities and Constraints of the Physical Workplace, in Hans Verhoeven, ed., *Proceedings of the World, the Workplace and We, the Worker: eWork in a Global World,* Brussels: International Trade Union, 2002.

Bikson, Tora K., and J. D. Everland, "Sociotechnical Reinvention: Implementation Dynamics and Collaboration Tools," *Information Communication & Society,* Vol. 1, No. 3, 1998, pp. 269–289.

Bikson, Tora K., and Constantijn W. A. Panis, *Citizens, Computers, and Connectivity: A Review of Trends,* Santa Monica, Calif.: RAND, MR-1109-MF, 1999.

Bikson, T. K., G. F. Treverton, J. Moini, and G. Lindstrom, *New Challenges for International Leadership: Lessons from Organizations with Global Missions,* Santa Monica, Calif.: RAND, MR-1670-IP, 2003.

Bradsher, Keith, "China Growth Leaves India Feeling Left Out," *International Herald Tribune,* November 30–December 1, 2002a, p. 12.

_____, "Indian State Chief's Business Savvy Lures Western Firms," *International Herald Tribune,* December 28–29, 2002b, p. 11.

Burkhart, Grey E., and Susan Older, *The Information Revolution in the Middle East and North Africa,* Santa Monica, Calif.: RAND, MR-1653-NIC, 2003.

BusinessWeek, "Special Report: Rethinking the Internet," March 26, 2001, pp. 116–141.

_____, "Special Report: A Mass Market of One," December 2, 2002a, pp. 68–72.

_____, "Greater China," December 9, 2002b, pp. 50–58.

Christensen, Clayton M., *The Innovator's Dilemma: When New Technologies Cause Great Firms to Fail,* Boston: Harvard Business School Press, 1997.

Connell, James, "Europe's 3G Hopes Fade," *International Herald Tribune,* August 30, 2002, p. 1.

Cook Network Consultants, *The Cook Report on the Internet,* Vol. 11, No. 10, January 2003.

Davis, Bob, "Past Crises Offer Hope for Economy, Warning to Watch," *Wall Street Journal,* September 26, 2002, p. A1.

Dewar, James A., "The Information Age and the Printing Press: Looking Backward to See Ahead," Santa Monica, Calif.: RAND, P-8014, 1998.

Donahue, John D., "The Start of Something Big? Predictions," in Elaine Ciulla Kamarck and Joseph S. Ney, Jr., eds., *democracy.com? Governance in a Networked World,* Hollis, N.H.: Hollis Publishing, 1999, pp. 193–196.

Drucker, Peter F., *The New Realities,* New York: Harper & Row, 1989.

_____, *Post-Capitalist Society,* New York: HarperCollins, 1993.

The Economist, "European Telecoms: Running for the Exit," August 16, 2001.

_____, "Mobile Telecoms: The Tortoise and the Hare," March 14, 2002a.

_____, "Special Report: The Telecoms Crisis," July 20, 2002b, pp. 59–61.

_____, "Night Fell on a Different World," September 7, 2002c, pp. 22–24.

_____, "The IMF: Doubts Inside the Barricades," September 28, 2002d, pp. 63–65.

Edwards, Gary, "Fear—Fight and Flight on the Corporate Battlefield: Can Open-Source Survive American Business?" *Darwin Magazine,* June 12, 2001.

Engardio, Pete, Aaron Bernstein, and Manjeet Kripalani, "Is Your Job Next?" *BusinessWeek,* February 3, 2003, pp. 50–59.

Enriquez, Juan, *As the Future Catches You,* New York: Crown Business, 2001.

Faiola, Anthony, "The Reason to Cry for Argentina," *International Herald Tribune,* August 7, 2002, p. 1.

Fairlamb, David, and Gail Edmondson, "Work in Progress: Signs Abound of a Nascent New Economy," *BusinessWeek,* January 31, 2000, pp. 80–87.

Fan, Ming, Sayee Srinivasan, Jan Stallaert, and Andrew B. Whinston, *Electronic Commerce and the Revolution in Financial Markets,* Cincinnati, Ohio: Thomson Learning, 2002.

Filkins, Dexter, "India's Office Pool," *Los Angeles Times,* April 6, 2000, p. A1.

Franda, Marcus, *Launching into Cyberspace: Internet Development and Politics in Five World Regions,* Boulder, Colo.: Lynne Rienner Publishers, 2002.

Friedman, Thomas L., *The Lexus and the Olive Tree,* New York: Farrar, Straus and Giroux, 1999.

Fukuyama, Francis, *Trust: The Social Virtues and the Creation of Prosperity,* New York: Simon & Schuster, 1995.

_____, "Europe and America: The West May Be Cracking," *International Herald Tribune*, Friday, August 9, 2002, p. 4.

Goodman, Seymour E., Grey E. Burkhart, William A. Foster, Laurence I. Press, Zixiang (Alex) Tan, and Jonathan Woodard, *The Global Diffusion of the Internet Project: An Initial Inductive Study*, Fairfax, Va.: The MOSAIC Group, March 1998.

Goodman, Peter S., "China Takes a Pivotal Role in High-Tech Production," *International Herald Tribune*, December 5, 2002, p. 2.

Grimond, John, "Survey: Japan," *The Economist*, April 18, 2002.

Grove, Andrew S., *Only the Paranoid Survive: How to Exploit the Crisis Points That Challenge Every Company and Career*, New York: Doubleday, 1996.

Hachigian, Nina, and Lily Wu, *The Information Revolution in Asia*, Santa Monica, Calif.: RAND, MR-1719-NIC, 2003.

Harrison, Lawrence E., and Samuel P. Huntington, eds., *Culture Matters: How Values Shape Human Progress*, New York: Basic Books, 2000.

Hill, Kevin A., and John E. Hughes, *Cyberpolitics: Citizen Activism in the Age of the Internet*, Lanham, Md.: Rowman & Littlefield, 1998.

Hillner, Jennifer, "Venture Capitals," *Wired*, No. 8.07, July 2000.

Hilsenrath, Jon E., "Sustainable Development Gains Cachet," *Wall Street Journal*, November 25, 2002, p. A2.

Hiltzik, Michael A., "Israel's High Tech Shifts into High Gear," *Los Angeles Times*, August 13, 2000, p. A1.

Hunaidi, Rima Khalaf, UNDP, United Nations, *Economic Development and Integration as a Catalyst for Peace*, testimony before the House International Relations Committee, July 24, 2002.

Hundley, Richard O., *Past Revolutions, Future Transformations: What Can the History of Revolutions in Military Affairs Tell Us About Transforming the U.S. Military*, Santa Monica, Calif.: RAND, MR-1029-DARPA, 1999.

Hundley, Richard O., Robert H. Anderson, Tora K. Bikson, James A. Dewar, Jerrold Green, Martin Libicki, and C. Richard Neu, *The Global Course of the Information Revolution: Political, Economic, and Social Consequences—Proceedings of an International Conference*, Santa Monica, Calif.: RAND, CF-154-NIC, 2000.

Hundley, Richard O., Robert H. Anderson, Tora K. Bikson, Maarten Botterman, Jonathan Cave, C. Richard Neu, Michelle Norgate, and Renée Cordes, *The Future of the Information Revolution in Europe: Proceedings of an International Conference*, Santa Monica, Calif.: RAND, CF-172-NIC, 2001.

Hurtig, Mel, *The Vanishing Country: Is It Too Late to Save Canada?* Toronto, Ontario: McClelland & Stewart, 2002.

International Telecommunication Union (ITU), *ITU Telecommunication Indicators Update: January-February-March 2001*, ITU Bureau of Telecommunication Development, March 2002.

Iritani, Evelyn, "Japan Giving Its Start-Ups a U.S. Education, with Limited Success," *Los Angeles Times*, September 10, 2000, p. C1.

Jones, R. J. Barry, *The World Turned Upside Down? Globalization and the Future of the State*, Manchester, United Kingdom, and New York: Manchester University Press, 2000.

Kamarck, Elaine Ciulla, "Political Campaigning on the Internet: Business as Usual?" in Elaine Ciulla Kamarck and Joseph S. Ney, Jr., eds., *Governance.com: Democracy in the Information Age*, Washington, D.C.: Brookings Institution Press, 2002, pp. 81–103.

Kamarck, Elaine Ciulla, and Joseph S. Ney, Jr., eds., *democracy.com? Governance in a Networked World*, Hollis, N.H.: Hollis Publishing, 1999.

_____, eds., *Governance.com: Democracy in the Information Age*, Washington, D.C.: Brookings Institution Press, 2002.

Kashkoul, Nabil M., and Molouk Y. Ba-Isa, "Toward the ICT Revolution," *Arab News*, May 26, 2002.

Kaufman, Jonathan, "After Years in the U.S., Mr. Luo Seeks Fortune in China," *Wall Street Journal*, March 6, 2003, p. A1.

Keohane, Robert O., and Joseph S. Nye, Jr., "Power and Interdependence in the Information Age," *Foreign Affairs,* Vol. 77, No. 5, September–October 1998.

King, David C., "Catching Voters in the Web," in Elaine Ciulla Kamarck and Joseph S. Ney, Jr., eds., *Governance.com: Democracy in the Information Age,* Washington, D.C.: Brookings Institution Press, 2002, pp. 104–116.

Kotkin, Joel, *The New Geography: How the Digital Revolution Is Reshaping the American Landscape,* New York: Random House, 2000.

Kraemer, Kenneth L., Jason Dedrick, and Debora Dunkle, *E-Commerce: A Mile Wide and an Inch Deep,* Irvine, Calif.: Center for Research on Information Technology and Organizations, University of California, Irvine, 2002.

Lee Kuan Yew, *From Third World to First, The Singapore Story: 1965–2000,* New York: HarperCollins, 2000.

Lessig, Lawrence, *The Future of Ideas: The Fate of the Commons in a Connected World,* New York: Random House, 2001.

Levine, Robert A., "Thinking Big," *The Milken Institute Review,* First Quarter 2001, pp. 81–87. Also available as Robert A. Levine, *Thinking Big,* Santa Monica, Calif.: RAND, RP-938, 2001.

Liebowitz, Stan J., *Re-Thinking the Network Economy: The True Forces That Drive the Digital Marketplace,* New York: American Management Association, 2002.

Lipschultz, David, "High Tech in Israel," *Red Herring,* September 1, 2000a.

_____, "Israel's Technology Sector Stands Strong," *Red Herring,* December 19, 2000b, pp. 36–37.

_____, "Born of Necessity: Brazil's Surprising Lead in E-Banking, *International Herald Tribune,* March 26, 2001.

Lipset, Seymour Martin, *American Exceptionalism: A Double-Edged Sword,* New York: W. W. Norton & Company, 1996.

Mann, Charles C., "Electronic Paper Turns the Page," *[MIT] Technology Review,* March 2001.

Mechling, Jerry, "Information Age Governance: Just the Start of Something Big?" in Elaine Ciulla Kamarck and Joseph S. Ney, Jr., eds., *Governance.com: Democracy in the Information Age,* Washington, D.C.: Brookings Institution Press, 2002, pp. 141–160.

Meyer-Larsen, Werner, *Germany, Inc.: The New German Juggernaut and Its Challenge to World Business,* New York: John Wiley & Sons, 2000.

Micklethwait, John, and Adrian Wooldridge, *A Future Perfect: The Challenge and Hidden Promise of Globalization,* London: William Heinemann, 2000.

Miles, James, "Survey: China," *The Economist,* June 13, 2002.

Miyashita, Hideo, "The Present Status and Characteristics of the Information Revolution in Japan," presentation at the RAND Conference on the Global Course of the Information Revolution: Political, Economic, and Social Consequences, Washington, D.C., November 16–18, 1999.

NAS/CSTB, *Information Technology in the Service Sector: A Twenty-First Century Lever,* National Research Council, Computer Science and Telecommunications Board, Washington, D.C.: National Academy Press, 1994.

National Intelligence Council (NIC), *Global Trends 2015: A Dialogue About the Future with Nongovernment Experts,* NIC 2000-02, December 2000.

_____, *Global Migration Trends and Their Implications for the United States: A National Intelligence Estimate,* 2001.

National Intelligence Council and State Department Bureau of Intelligence and Research (NIC/State Department), *Workshop on Information Technology in Africa, Conference Proceedings, 2–3 October 2001,* Report CR 2002-01, May 2002.

National Nanotechnology Initiative: Leading to the Next Industrial Revolution, Executive Office of the President of the United States, February 7, 2000.

National Science Foundation and Department of Commerce (NSF/DOC) *Converging Technologies for Improving Human Performance,* June 2002.

Norris, Pippa, "Revolution, What Revolution? The Internet and U.S. Elections, 1992–2000," in Elaine Ciulla Kamarck and Joseph S. Ney, Jr., eds., *Governance.com: Democracy in the Information Age,* Washington, D.C.: Brookings Institution Press, 2002, pp. 59–80.

Nye, Jr., Joseph S., "Information Technology and Democratic Governance," in Elaine Ciulla Kamarck and Joseph S. Ney, Jr., eds., *Governance.com: Democracy in the Information Age,* Washington, D.C.: Brookings Institution Press, 2002, pp. 1–16.

Oakes, Chris, "Successful e-Commerce Means Going Back to Basics," *International Herald Tribune,* June 24, 2002, p. 12.

Ohmae, Kenichi, *The End of the Nation State,* New York: The Free Press, 1995.

Ono, Yumiko, and Bill Spindle, "Standing Along—Japan's Long Decline Makes One Thing Rise: Individualism," *Wall Street Journal,* December 30, 2000, p. A1.

Organisation for Economic Co-operation and Development (OECD), *Measuring the Information Economy,* 2002.

Pacific Council on International Policy (PCIP), The Working Group on E-Government in the Developing World, *Roadmap for E-Government in the Developing World,* April 2002.

Peet, John, "Survey: E-Commerce," *The Economist,* February 26, 2000.

Porter, Michael E., "Clusters and the New Economics of Competition," *Harvard Business Review,* November–December, 1998, pp. 77–90.

The President's Commission on Critical Infrastructure Protection (PCCIP), *Critical Foundations: Protecting America's Infrastructures,* October 1997.

The President's Critical Infrastructure Protection Board (PCIPB), *The National Strategy to Secure Cyberspace,* September 2002.

Rai, Saritha, "India Is Regaining Contracts with U.S.," *New York Times,* December 25, 2002, p. W1.

Ranadivé, Vivek, *The Power of Now,* New York: McGraw-Hill, 1999.

Red Herring, "Special China Report," November 2002, pp. 33–44.

Reich, Robert B., *The Work of Nations,* New York: Alfred A. Knopf, 1991.

Roland-Holst, David, *An Overview of PRC's Emergence and East Asian Trade Patterns to 2020,* ADB Institute Research Paper Series No. 44, Asian Development Bank, October 2002.

Romero, Simon, "Net Calling Gets Out of Its Niche," *International Herald Tribune,* January 7, 2003, p. 11.

Scherer, Frederic M., *Innovation and Growth: Schumpeterian Perspectives,* Cambridge, Mass.: MIT Press, 1984.

Schumpeter, Joseph A., *The Theory of Economic Development,* Cambridge, Mass.: Harvard University Press, 1934.

_____, *Capitalism, Socialism, and Democracy,* New York and London: Harper & Brothers, 1942.

Sender, Henny, "Soaring Indian Tech Salaries Reflect the Country's Brain Drain," *Wall Street Journal,* August 21, 2000, p. A13.

Shapiro, Carl, and Hal R. Varian, *Information Rules: A Strategic Guide to the Network Economy,* Boston: Harvard Business School Press, 1999.

Shionoya, Yuichi, and Mark Perlman, eds., *Innovation in Technology, Industries, and Institutions: Studies in Schumpeterian Perspectives,* Ann Arbor, Mich.: University of Michigan Press, 1994.

Shiver, Jube, Jr., "Alliance Fights Boost in Visas for Tech Workers," *Los Angeles Times,* August 5, 2000, p. C1.

Siegele, Ludwig, "Survey: The Real-Time Economy," *The Economist,* January 31, 2002.

Simon, Leslie David, Javier Corrales, and Donald R. Wolfensberger, *Democracy and the Internet: Allies or Adversaries?* Washington, D.C.: Woodrow Wilson Center Press, 2002.

Spar, Debora L., *Ruling the Waves: Cycles of Discovery, Chaos, and Wealth Form the Compass to the Internet,* New York: Harcourt, 2001.

Stone, Amey, "Wi-Fi: It's Fast, It's Here—and It Works," *Business-Week Online,* April 1, 2002.

Strange, Susan, *The Retreat of the State,* Cambridge, United Kingdom: Cambridge University Press, 1996.

Sugarman, Margo Lipschitz, "The Virtual World of Yossi Vardi," *The Jerusalem Report,* May 22, 2000, pp. 44–47.

Symonds, Matthew, "Survey: Business and the Internet," *The Economist,* June 24, 1999.

Tempest, Rone, "China Woos Back Its Silicon Valley Set," *International Herald Tribune,* November 27, 2002, p. 1.

Thompson, Dennis, "James Madison on Cyberdemocracy," in Elaine Ciulla Kamarck and Joseph S. Ney, Jr., eds., *Governance.com: Democracy in the Information Age,* Washington, D.C.: Brookings Institution Press, 2002, pp. 32–39.

Throsby, David, *Economics and Culture,* Cambridge, United Kingdom: Cambridge University Press, 2001.

Toffler, Alvin, *Future Shock,* Mattituck, N.Y.: Amereon, 1970.

Treverton, Gregory F., and Lee Mizell, *The Future of the Information Revolution in Latin America: Proceedings of an International Conference,* Santa Monica, Calif.: RAND, CF-166-1-NIC, 2001.

Trofimov, Yaroslav, "Lifting the Veil: In a Quiet Revolution, Qatar Is Snubbing Neighboring Saudis," *Wall Street Journal*, October 24, 2002, p. A1.

United Nations Development Programme (UNDP), *Human Development Report 2001: Making New Technologies Work for Human Development*, 2001.

_____, *Arab Human Development Report 2002: Creating Opportunities for Future Generations*, 2002.

Verhovek, Sam Howe, "Bill Gates Turns Skeptical on Digital Solution's Scope," *New York Times*, November 3, 2000, p. A18.

"Where the U.S. Is Getting High-Tech Help," *Los Angeles Times*, August 5, 2000, p. C1.

Wilson, Ernest, *The Information Revolution in Developing Countries*, Boston: MIT Press, 2003.

Wolcott, Peter, *The Diffusion of the Internet in the Republic of Turkey*, Stanford, Calif.: Consortium for Research on Information Security and Policy (CRISP), Stanford University, 1999.

Wolcott, Peter, Seymour Goodman, and Gary Burkhart, *The Information Technology Capability of Nations: A Framework for Analysis*, Stanford, Calif.: Center for International Security and Arms Control, Stanford University, January 1997.